MY LOST POETS

MY LOST POETS

A LIFE IN POETRY

PHILIP LEVINE

EDITED BY EDWARD HIRSCH

ALFRED A. KNOPF · NEW YORK · 2018

This Is a Borzoi Book
Published by Alfred A. Knopf

Copyright © 2016 by The Estate of Philip Levine
All rights reserved. Published in the United States by Alfred A. Knopf,
a division of Penguin Random House LLC, New York, and distributed
in Canada by Random House of Canada, a division of Penguin Random
House Canada Limited, Toronto.

www.aaknopf.com

Knopf, Borzoi Books, and the colophon are registered trademarks of
Penguin Random House LLC.

Pages 207–210 constitute an extension of the copyright page.

Library of Congress Cataloging-in-Publication Data
Names: Levine, Philip, 1928–2015, author.
Title: My lost poets : a life in poetry / Philip Levine.
Description: New York : Alfred A. Knopf, 2016. |
Includes bibliographical references.
Identifiers: LCCN 2016022244 | ISBN 9780451493279 (hardcover) |
ISBN 9780451493293 (ebook) | ISBN 9781524711337 (trade pbk.)
Subjects: LCSH: Poetry—Authorship. | Poetry—Influence. | Influence
(Literary, artistic, etc.) | Levine, Philip, 1928–2015. | Levine, Philip, 1928–
2015—Friends and associates. | Poets, American—20th century—Biography.
| BISAC: LITERARY COLLECTIONS / Essays. | POETRY / American /
General. | BIOGRAPHY & AUTOBIOGRAPHY / Personal Memoirs.
Classification: LCC PS3562.E9 A6 2016 | DDC 811/.54 [B]—dc23
LC record available at https://lccn.loc.gov/2016022244

Cover photograph by CoverZoo/Alamy
Cover design by Chip Kidd

Manufactured in the United States of America
Published November 9, 2016
First Paperback Edition

CONTENTS

Foreword vii

MY LOST POETS 3

NOBODY'S DETROIT 37

ON FINDING WILLIAM CARLOS WILLIAMS
AND MY POETRY 53

DETROIT JAZZ IN THE LATE FORTIES
AND EARLY FIFTIES 59

A HISTORY OF MY BEFUDDLEMENT 79

A DAY IN MAY 101

A MEANS OF TRANSPORT:
GEORGE HITCHCOCK AND *kayak* 123

THE SPANISH CIVIL WAR IN POETRY 135

IN THE NEXT WORLD:
THE POETRY OF ROBERTA SPEAR 165

GETTING AND SPENDING 179

Acknowledgments 205

FOREWORD

Philip Levine's prose is an extension of his poetry. It shows his unwavering purpose, his characteristic values and commitments, his lifelong tenacities. Same obsessions, different delivery systems. He was always faithful to what he cared for and believed in. The voice in all of his work is unmistakable—refreshingly direct, bracingly honest—though here it is a little more relaxed and sociable than in his poems. He is more willing to explain things, to show the literary side of his sensibility, and his wide-ranging poetic education. Many of the pieces in this book display his appreciation of other poets, his former students, his contemporaries, but also his necessary precursors, those who influenced him, such as Keats and Lorca, as well as some of his important teachers, especially Berryman. "My Lost Poets," a lecture he delivered as poet laureate at the Library of Congress, gives us the fullest and most revealing account of how he came to be a poet, his turbulent adolescence in Detroit, his key years as a college student at Wayne University. "I composed my first poems in the dark," he writes. This essay is one of the great textured descriptions of a writer finding his vocation.

Philip Levine was working on this book, which he titled *My Lost Poets,* until his death. Along with the title piece, he designated four other essays for this volume: "Nobody's Detroit," "In the Next World: The Poetry of Roberta Spear," "A Day in May," and "A Means of Transport: George Hitchcock and *kayak*." We have supplemented these essays with several pieces that speak to his most enduring concerns: "On Finding William Carlos Williams and My Poetry"; "Detroit

Jazz in the Late Forties and Early Fifties," which he created in correspondence with Sascha Feinstein for the magazine *Brilliant Corners;* "A History of My Befuddlement," which he gave as a lecture on the teaching of poetry and subsequently published in *Five Points;* "Getting and Spending," which he first presented as a talk at the Chicago Humanities Festival; and "The Spanish Civil War in Poetry," which he delivered as a lecture at the University of California, Berkeley. He included poems, both his own and others', in some of his lectures, thus uniting the two strands of his work. The lectures are fascinating in their own right, but they also cast a keen light on his practice as a poet. Meant for a live audience, they are often hilariously funny, as he was, but also deeply serious. All of his prose works are rescue operations. They are ferociously loyal to the past.

In this book, Levine often makes little distinction between poets he read on the page and those he knew in life. They were all equally real to him, his comrades in poetry. For all of his ironies, he had a sustaining belief in his vocation. That's why the first piece here rises to such a rapturous conclusion, gathering up his dead, those who had inspired him, and thus come to inspire us:

> Back then I didn't know just how much I needed
> them or how much they'd already given me. I needed
> not merely their encouragement, their criticism, their
> intelligence and dedication and their soulfulness—
> for these were powerfully soulful people—and
> their fellowship in our ancient discipline. I think
> more than anything I needed their belief that we
> would share in the singular glory of poetry. Where
> would I have been without that belief, without
> Bernard, Ruby, Paul, and Ulysses, my comrades

whose words inspired me, whose belief in me kept me going. Where would I have been without all of them, without Capetanakis and his strange vision of our origins, without Alun Lewis and the songs he hurled in death's face, without Replansky and her righteous indignation, her struggle to resurrect the true Americas of William Blake and César Vallejo, without the calm and surgical poems of Keith Douglas, without the dreams of all my lost or forgotten poets, my brothers and sisters in madness and glory who shared with me their faith in the power of the perfect words, the words we knew as children and then forgot?

EDWARD HIRSCH

MY LOST POETS

MY LOST POETS

I composed my first poems in the dark. In fact in the "double dark": that is, at night in a small woods that only the moon lit and also totally without the guidance or knowledge or light, if you will, that great or good or even mediocre poetry might have given me. In truth I never thought of these early compositions as poems; I never thought of them as anything but what they were: secret little speeches addressed to the moon when the moon was visible and when the moon was not visible to all those parts of creation that crowded around and above me as well as those parts that eluded me, the parts I had no name for, no notion of except for the fact they were listening.

I was fourteen years old and living for the first time on the outskirts of my city, Detroit, in an almost completely undeveloped area that still contained the trees and untended undergrowth a boy could transform in his imagination into an untamed wilderness. If you stood in the crotch of a copper beech and inhaled the thick atmosphere after rain or just before rain and closed your eyes you might come to believe you were in that fabled garden we were given and later lost, and you might want to speak to all the wonders of our human inheritance, you might even want to say thanks for being a creation in a world of other creations. You might want no longer to be alone and misunderstood, and for that you needed poetry.

Sadly enough I did not know poetry although it was on hand. Had I gone to the bookshelf in our tiny study at home I could have taken down a volume of Robert Service and read in galloping, rhymed lines how a plucky boy no older than I had killed his Prussian tormentor, a sadistic major, or better still my mother's favorite poet, Francis Thompson, whose "The Hound of Heaven" she would declaim on nights the phone didn't ring or she had no gentlemen callers. How she loved those lines:

> *I fled Him, down the nights and down the days;*
> *I fled Him, down the arches of the years;*
> *I fled Him, down the labyrinthine ways*
> *Of my own mind, and in the midst of tears*
> *I hid from Him, and under running laughter.*

The flight goes on—"Adown Titanic glooms of chasmed fears"—for a couple hundred more lines and ends in an embrace. I'd been hearing the poem since I was seven or eight and it wasn't getting better. Boys that age are tough critics and savage when it comes to the taste of their parents. If that was poetry I didn't need it.

What were my models for my dark-time psalms? Let me describe my compositions: they were Whitmanian without the benefit of Whitman. That good gray, gay poet was not taught in the Detroit public schools, at least not in those I attended. And no living poet was taught, not even the poet laureate of Michigan; I refer to our newspaper poet Edgar A. Guest, who gave us the immortal, oft-quoted "It takes a heap o' livin' in a house t'make it home." (Somehow "the People's Poet," as he was then called, never made the snooty anthologies, though his work still appears in *Reader's Digest*.) Who was taught in my schools? We memorized a sixty-line passage from the prologue to *The Canterbury Tales* and also stunning passages from *Macbeth,* but you had to have the genius of John Keats to accept such giants as an influence, and even at fourteen I knew I was not a genius.

Let me be clear: I had no idea that I was writing poetry—and of course I wasn't—; so let me put it another way, no notion that I was trying to write poetry. I began this solitary in-the-dark process—which would last some years—without its ever occurring to me that I was attempting poetry. I simply had no name for what I was doing, but even without a category to place these experiments in I found them incredibly satisfying. At the time I knew exactly why they thrilled me. I had discovered a voice within myself I'd had no idea had been there, a voice that could speak of all the things I would never have dared share with anyone, a voice that tried to consider the value of being alive, the sense of what it was to be alive, not so much as Philip Levine or any other Levine or any other Philip, just to be alive. Everything I composed was joyous as though there were not a skeptical thought in my mind. Yet in my daily dealings with the world I was a teenager, a skeptical, at times even cynical teenager, just as most of you were all those years ago. I did not then know that the work ahead—the writing of poetry—would take years, that what I had begun almost by chance in the crotch of a copper beech would become the work of my lifetime, what I would labor to perfect for seventy years and always fail to reach a perfection. Nor did I know that in order to bring that work to any satisfactory level I would need help from sources I did not know existed.

11

Not all teenagers are skeptical or cynical. As a somewhat older teenager—nineteen to be exact, in the spring of 1947—I attended my first poetry reading. It was held in a small room in Webster Hall of Wayne University, and it began at a few minutes after one p.m. The seven readers were university students and two faculty members. I'd seen an announcement of the event in the school newspaper and my curiosity was aroused. I remember almost nothing of the event except for one line of verse and one fact. The fact: there existed in the school library something called the Miles Poetry Room, which held a significant collection of twentieth-century poetry, once the library of Theodore Miles, an aspiring poet and former faculty member who'd died while serving in the navy in the Pacific during World War II. The line: "When in a mirror love redeems my eyes," the opening line of a poem recited by its author, Bernard Strempek, a tall, loose-limbed boy with the hurt face of a fallen angel—he looked no older than fifteen. The recitation was in a voice the likes of which I'd never heard in all my wanderings through Detroit. How to describe it? A cross between a high-tenor version of Cary Grant and the call to arms of a mad warrior in a great human struggle, a John Brown or Joan of Arc voice. Whoever this Strempek was, he was overpoweringly serious about what he regarded as poetry. Why that one line? I was struck by this boy's willingness to openly acknowledge his narcissism, and I loved the music and movement of the line, the way the iambics began surprisingly and turned to a flow that crashed on the shore of the word "love." I'd never attempted such mastery of rhythm; in my writing I was concerned with narrative and imagery. I so worried Strempek's single line in my head that most of the rest of that poem and the poems of the other poets passed as noise. I was too shy and/or too humbled by these brazen poets to attempt to speak to anyone there: I went home totally confused by the experience. There was a third fact far more meaningful than the other two: there were living poets in my town, some my own age and at least one younger, and no matter how well or how badly they wrote they were serious about a life in poetry. I was not alone.

The next Monday afternoon I decided to visit this new discovery, the Miles Poetry Room. At the time the university library was housed in the second floor of Old Main, a stately four-story Gothic building that once housed Central High School before there was a city university. The room itself was a comfortable one, with battered armchairs, two sagging couches, and high windows that looked out on a good deal of auto and truck traffic, but a quiet room nonetheless. On that first occasion I encountered a single reader, whom I immediately recognized as young Strempek. I picked a book from the shelves—there were literally hundreds of books—and pretended to read. Suddenly Strempek turned to me and said, "Listen to this, I've discovered a new master," and he read from a slender collection: "My brother, Cain, the wounded . . ." And paused. "What an amazing opening! Why didn't I think of it?" I was surprised to discover his speaking voice was the same as his formal presentation voice, the same original accent, the same quavering seriousness that seemed to say, "Yes, I am a Poet—don't fool with me!" "This is a discovery for me," he said. "Do you have any brothers?" I did. "Then this poem was written for you," and he handed me the book as he rose to leave.

ABEL

My brother, Cain, the wounded, liked to sit
Brushing my shoulder, by the staring water
Of life or death, in cinemas half-lit
By scenes of peace that always turned to slaughter.

He liked to talk to me. His eager voice
Whispered the puzzle of his bleeding thirst,
Or prayed to me not to make my final choice
Unless we had a chat about it first.

And then he chose the final pain for me.
I do not blame his nature: he's my brother;
Nor what you call the times: our love was free,
Would be at any time, but rather

The ageless ambiguity of things
Which makes our life mean death, our love be hate.
My blood that streams across the bedroom sings,
"I am my brother opening the gate!"

DEMETRIOS CAPETANAKIS (1912–1944)

At the time I had no idea this poem would stay with me for the rest of my life, as would the memory of that encounter with this original and generous young man. I called him a boy earlier, and he was: he was seventeen years old, majoring in French, which he spoke fluently. When, later, I asked him why French, I got a one-word answer, "Rimbaud," for the boy genius of French poetry was his idol and along with Hart Crane the model for his poetry and, unfortunately, his life.

And who was Capetanakis, and why did this poem stick to me for over sixty years? He was born in Smyrna in 1912, studied economics at the University of Athens, and later received a doctorate in philosophy from Heidelberg. He came to England in 1939 on a scholarship from Cambridge and almost immediately became a protégé of Edith Sitwell. Whatever small recognition Capetanakis got, it was due to the efforts of the writer and editor John Lehmann, who became his close friend and published him in his magazine *New Writing*. After the poet's death of leukemia in 1944, Lehmann brought out a collection of his writing in English under the title *Demetrios Capetanakis: A Greek Poet in England*. The volume is largely essays on literary figures, including Rimbaud, Dostoyevsky, Proust, Thomas Gray, and William Plomer, as well as translations of contemporary Greek poets and sixteen of his own original poems written in English.

To return to Bernie Strempek's question sixty-some years later, yes, I have brothers, and one is a twin, an identical twin brother who still resembles me physically and perhaps in other ways, but I don't think one needs a brother to be struck by the poem "Abel." In fact all one needs is an ear to hear it and the knowledge that brother killing brother is one of the oldest and saddest truths of human mythology and history. At nineteen I'd never heard or read a poem that re-created a mythic character's speech in contemporary English. Not only does Abel use the words I might have used if I had been more fluent and accomplished, he says things I might say, for I also saw those scenes of "peace that always turned to slaughter" in the films of that day—or, for that matter, the films of this day. At the time I had recently stumbled into modern and modernist poetry, so the whole question of form was utterly new and confusing to me. So much of what I read was inspiring and incomprehensible that I was both lost and found: found in that the language of Yeats, Eliot, Pound, Crane, Auden, Dylan Thomas was thrilling, and lost when I attempted to discern what they were writing about. Out of necessity I had adopted a mantra I'd found in an essay by T. S. Eliot: one understands a poem before one understands a poem, one gets it in the gut and the rational understanding eventually follows. (Of course Eliot didn't write exactly that, but that was the useful and self-serving translation by Phil for Phil. This might have been true for Eliot, but in my case—no doubt many cases—a prolonged wait of perhaps sixty years or more has not brought rational understanding to a good deal of what confused me then.) The poem "Abel," however, puzzled me not at all. It was written during the dark days of World War II in a country under siege, and it finds the root of the horror in an eternal and intimate relationship in which love turns to hate. For Capetanakis the wounded one is Cain, the victim of his own circumstance and nature. The tragedy of the book of Genesis is reenacted in a bedroom, my bedroom or yours, in 1940 or tomorrow. As far as I can recall, what I reacted to sixty years ago was the language and the imagery; the phrasing for the most part appeared to me to be casual, almost offhand, but the diction is so precisely there that I found myself memorizing the poem effortlessly and at first believing the poem was transparent, only later questioning what the conclusion could possibly mean, with its blood that sings and the anthem that it sings in this domestic setting, "I am my brother opening the gate!" I learned to love the mystery of it, and I still do. I was also learning to take pleasure in the mystery of poetry and not to constantly demand an understanding of the poet's world or my world: to paraphrase Keats, I was not beset with an irritable searching after final truths. Already the Keats I'd found in his amazing letters was becoming—and still remains—a guiding compass.

I I I

The first true poet who mattered to me was Wilfred Owen, the poet of the Great War who died in action on the Western Front a week before the armistice. My marvelous high-school literature teacher, Mrs. Paperno, one afternoon read the class Owen's poem "Arms and the Boy." This took place in the autumn of '44, and most of the boys in class expected to be drafted as soon as they graduated. How Mrs. Paperno divined that I was a secret poet I don't know, but for some reason she asked me after class if I'd like to borrow the book over the weekend. She would let me take it if I promised to wear white gloves whilst reading it. Huh? I said. "It's a metaphor, Philip," she said. "Don't spill soup on it." Why did Owen's poems matter so much? I suppose it was the first time I'd encountered in print attitudes like my own toward that war—or any war. Only in secret did I admit to myself that I lived in dread—at the time a shameful dread—of the waiting combat. We were all taught to feel quite differently, that it might be a privilege to fight and die for our country; that was the constant background music to our coming of age, except in the classrooms of plucky Mrs. Paperno, who seemed determined to ready us for the lives we might actually live. Owen, however, had no influence on what I wrote at seventeen. His often exalted diction was not mine, the wizardry of his craft was utterly beyond me, and in the poems there was such wisdom earned through experience, I was simply left in awe.

In describing the inner life of one who survives the hell of war, he wrote:

> *Alive, he is not vital overmuch;*
> *Dying, not mortal overmuch,*
> *Nor sad, nor proud,*
> *Nor curious at all.*
> *He cannot tell*
> *Old men's placidity from his.*

If ever I knew this, I learned it from his poetry. Owen, of course, is not a lost poet. Even after his mental breakdown in 1917 (then called "shell shock") and before he went back to the front to die, his poems had been read and praised by two official soldier-poets of the day, Robert Graves and Siegfried Sassoon. Sassoon—who was the more celebrated of the two—tells us in a memoir that he knew immediately Owen's war poems were better than his own. Today Owen is regarded by many as the greatest war poet in our language. I was obsessed by the poetry of war, especially the English poetry of the two wars, perhaps because one of the few facts I knew regarding my father's life—he died when I was five—was that he had enlisted in the English army in 1916, though why he did this I never learned.

In the Miles Poetry Room I went hunting for more war poetry. The books were everywhere, and in a great jumble; there was no catalogue to tell where anything was. Since I had no idea what names or books to look for, I found the situation perfect. I just worked my way through the shelves and the piles left on tables and chairs and found what I wanted or didn't. And then I made a most singular discovery: a tiny, cheaply printed, badly bound wartime English edition of poetry with an astounding title, *Ha! Ha! Among the Trumpets* (a line, I later learned, from the book of Job, describing the cry of the warhorse as he charges into battle). The book was published by Allen & Unwin of London, with an introduction by Robert Graves. In fact there were two copies, and neither had ever been checked out. (One, I am ashamed to admit, is now in my study in Fresno.) It was authored by a Welsh poet, Alun Lewis, who'd died in Burma before the book was published in 1945. All these years later the poet is still largely unknown in our country. Like Owen, Lewis was an army lieutenant; like Owen, he chose to go to war only to discover he did not belong there—no one belonged there; and like Owen he failed to survive the war. But his poetry is nothing like Owen's, or for that matter like that of any of the well-known English poets of the Great War—Sassoon, Graves, Isaac Rosenberg, Ivor Gurney. For one thing it does not contain scenes of combat and slaughter; for another, it is largely a demotic poetry, and at its best personal and intimate. For some reason he'd felt obligated to enlist to defend his England, just as Edward Thomas had done twenty years before and so deprived us of more of his great poems. Like Edward Thomas, he was well married, but unlike Thomas, he lived long enough to regret his decision to enlist. His first foreign and final posting was India, and it was from there he wrote a letter home defining his spiritual and ethical situation: "I find myself quite unable to express at once the passion of Love, the coldness of Death (Death is cold), and the fire that beats against resignation, 'acceptance.' Acceptance seems so spiritless, protest so vain. In between the two I live." And though his work is humble, he is able to amass enormous rhythmic power that can transform his usual voice into one of oracular power and mystery. He was Welsh, and perhaps he carried in his blood or his memory the music of a bardic tradition; you can hear it in his astonishing poem "Song, on seeing dead bodies floating off the cape."

S O N G

(On seeing dead bodies floating off the Cape)

The first month of his absence
I was numb and sick
And where he'd left his promise
Life did not turn or kick.
The seed, the seed of love was sick.

The second month my eyes were sunk
In the darkness of despair,
And my bed was like a grave
And his ghost was lying there.
And my heart was sick with care.

The third month of his going
I thought I heard him say
"Our course deflected slightly
On the thirty-second day—"
The tempest blew his words away.

And he was lost among the waves,
The ship rolled helpless in the sea,
The fourth month of his voyage
He shouted grievously
"Beloved, do not think of me."

The flying fish like kingfishers
Skim the sea's bewildered crests,

The whales blow steaming fountains,
The sea-gulls have no nests
Where my lover sways and rests.

We never thought to buy or sell
This life that blooms or withers in the leaf,
And I'll not stir, so he sleeps well,
Though cell by cell the coral reef
Builds an eternity of grief.

But oh! the drag and dullness of my Self;
The turning seasons wither in my head;
All this slowness, all this hardness,
The nearness that is waiting in my bed,
The gradual self-effacement of the dead.

The death the woman foresees is not an ordinary death; it is epic, as epic as her loss. The great seas and the beasts of the seas and the birds of the air witness it in a state of shock. And yet life goes on as it must. Lewis does something amazing: he creates a dialogue between two lovers separated by thousands of miles and even further separated by their conditions, for one is living and one is dead. But of course the only dialogue is in the head of the survivor, who re-creates her lover, who then asks her to do exactly what she must but cannot yet do: forget him. But we know eventually she will—with his help—for it has already begun with "the gradual self-effacement of the dead." The poem ends with a profound psychological insight, for in fact the dead don't efface themselves; they don't need to. We do it for them. Without the least apology, Lewis has taken up the voice of a woman and assumed the knowledge of her grief, her double grief, for she is both barren and widowed. Such nerve! I thought, and today, with all our quarrels about gender identity, it feels even more nervy. What might Alun Lewis have written, I thought then and think now, had war not devoured him?

A few days later I caught my boy guru, Strempek, in the Miles Poetry Room, and handed him the book, open to "Song." Instead of reading it silently he stood and declaimed it almost entirely from memory, for he scarcely looked at the book. And there was that voice again, both trembling and commanding. When he'd finished, the two other students present stood and applauded; I'd discovered he read aloud the poems of others better than his own work. "There should be more of this in our poetry, especially in war poetry," he said. I asked him what he meant by "this," and my mentor again said a single word: "tenderness." I had never in my life known or even guessed there would be room for tenderness in great poetry, but the moment he used the word my mind began roaming over the poems I knew best, and of course he was right: there wasn't nearly enough. He asked me if I knew Lewis's poem "Goodbye." I didn't. "It's a soldier's love poem," he said, "I think I can do the final stanzas," and once again he declaimed from memory:

> Everything we renounce except ourselves;
> Selfishness is the last of all to go;
> Our sighs are exhalations of the earth,
> Our footprints leave a track across the snow.
>
> We made the universe to be our home,
> Our nostrils took the wind to be our breath,
> Our hearts are massive towers of delight,
> We stride across the seven seas of death.

Yet when all's done you'll keep the emerald
I placed upon your finger in the street;
And I will keep the patches that you sewed
On my old battledress tonight, my sweet.

Bernard was quiet for a moment, and then he said, "Can you just imagine one of us saying 'my sweet' in a poem? We just don't have the nerve. The great poets can say anything, use any word."

Curious it was that we never questioned the usefulness of hunting down poetry that suited our taste. Somehow we merely assumed that our immersion in poetry, true poetry, would benefit our own work as well as magically benefit us, our lives, our characters, our sense of self. I never talked about this with the other poets who gathered once a month in the Miles Poetry Room, for I was now an habitué, and in truth I have no idea how the others felt. It's very possible they were as naive as I. It was lovely to think I was becoming a better human being merely by poring over great poetry and stealing everything that suited me and hiding it in my poems where any knowledgeable reader would see it. At our meetings we read each other's work and except for Strempek we handled the poems of others very gingerly. I suspect we needed refuge in this huge, tough city so indifferent to our occupation. Bernard—utterly sure of his future in literature—said exactly what he believed, and we let him get away with it. Perhaps we needed one brilliant and brainy brat to tell us where we were. His own work had no fear of using a vocabulary I would never have dared employ, but in fact it was the language of his usual discourse, although he did not ordinarily speak in iambic pentameter; but yes, he often wrote in it, as in these lines he once recited in the Miles Poetry Room:

On this poised moment turning, I consider
You, the world, whose veins like strings accord
The instrument you live, and grace
Though you remember finer chords
Like choirs diminishing streams,
The discords which my hands convey.

Fifteen years after his drowning, Hart Crane resurfaced in the poetry of a Detroit teenager intoxicated by language. It's a pity Crane didn't stay around long enough to discover how great a gift his poetry was to the generations that followed.

I V

The regulars at the monthly Miles meetings included four World War II vets, none of whom were students and one of whom—Robert Huff—had appeared regularly in *Harper's, Poetry,* and *The Atlantic.* Another—Dudley Randall—would soon found a superb publishing house for poetry, the Broadside Press. Another—a student, Paul Petrie—would soon be drafted for the Korean War, and would, amazingly, return more dedicated than ever to becoming a serious poet. Our one elderly sage was Dick Werry, the single Wayne faculty member who regularly attended the meetings. The rest of us were students, and it was to one of these—Ruby Teague of Berea, Kentucky—I owed my discovery of the poetry of Naomi Replansky. I'm not sure where she found the poem she loaned me; it had been copied, she told me, from its presentation in a "literary periodical," to quote her accurately. (What she meant was she'd typed it out for me.) This was 1948, and four years would pass before Replansky's first book, *Ring Song,* appeared. Here is the title poem as Ruby handed it to me [slightly different from the printed version]:

RING SONG

When that joy is gone for good
I move the arms beneath the blood.

When the blood is running wild
I sew the clothing of a child.

When that child is never born
I lean my breast against a thorn.

When the thorn brings no reprieve
I rise and live, I rise and live.

When I live from hand to hand
Nude in the marketplace I stand.

When I stand and am not sold
I build a fire against the cold.

When the cold comes creeping round
I seek a warmer stamping-ground.

When that ground becomes too small
I come against a stony wall.

When that wall is not to climb
I chalk on it a burning rhyme.

When the rhyme can work no spell
I knew the circle of my hell.

When my hell does not destroy
I leap from ambush on my joy.

Reading it sixty-some years later, I hear clearly why Ruby chose it and why it gave me such delight. Replansky does something I never dared to do: she writes in the shadow of a great poet, William Blake, and she makes not the least effort to hide her allegiance. In his great poem "Auguries of Innocence" Blake used the same couplet form to utter his poetic truths: "The Bat that flits at close of Eve / Has left the Brain that wont Believe," "He who shall hurt the little Wren / Shall never be belov'd by men." Replansky has modeled her poem on exactly the right poem, for her "Ring Song" is an utterly innocent poem and an utterly original one; the child is alive in Replansky, alive and in control of the poem. She goes even farther: she marries Blake to surrealism. She might well have known the work of David Gascoyne (". . . the drums of the hospitals were broken like glass / and glass were the faces in the last looking-glass"—that from Gascoyne's "And the Seventh Dream Is the Dream of Isis"), then the outstanding surrealist poet in English. And for flavor Replansky adds a sprig of Mother Goose, so that this tough and visionary poem feels completely good-natured. Auden was doing something similar in his ballad poems written in the forties, when "Ring Song" was also written; but Auden was one of the major stars in the firmament of poetry in English and the book *Ring Song* was a first book—a remarkable first book, nominated for the National Book Award, but still a first book, with the charm that first books often have, with their lack of cohesion and any defense system as the poems fly off in different directions, sometimes arriving at beauty and other times arriving at cliché. At the time—1948—I do not believe I understood the perfect justice that Ruby Teague, a gracious rural Southern Baptist, should bring me the gift of a poem by Replansky, a New York Jewish leftist. The truth is, Ruby was not who I thought she was; I was put off by her manners, her genteel speech, her looks. She turned out to be a warrior for human dignity, and Replansky was her poet.

Ruby was both surprised and delighted by my response; she'd given this very copy to Bernard. Oh, yes, he'd read it, and labeled it "kid stuff." I was more than a little surprised, for with his obsession with French poetry he must have known at least some of the work of the surrealists, Breton and company. It turned out he did know their work, had once admired it, but his "sensibility" had "matured"—he actually used those words. In fact, except for Apollinaire, he told me, he had little use for twentieth-century French poetry. Looking back on it, I'm amazed we let Bernard play the role of Dr. Johnson; perhaps someone had to, and he derived so much pleasure from his pronouncements it seemed churlish to deny him. By this time I knew he was playing a part—the boy poetry wonder and the sage of Motor City—and the rest of us pretended to require his counsel. And of course I now recognize he was laughing at himself—and, I suppose, at us.

A few days later Ruby brought me a second poem by Replansky, clearly the work of the same poetic imagination, and yet a remarkably different poem: one that enacts a small drama before our eyes, with characters formed out of nature and dreams—a tree, a river, a child, a word—brought together by the poet for a singular ritual.

THE SONG THAT WENT ON
DURING THE TRAGEDY

"Let them not bother me,"
said the tree by the river.
"Why do they bother me
with their howling by the river?"

"Let her not carry me,"
said the child deep inside.
"Why does she carry me
with that sorrow deep inside?"

"Let him not utter me,"
said the word in the throat.
"Why does he utter me
as though I blistered his throat?"

But he in his shouting,
and she in her fury,
they never heard,
how could they hear

the word in the throat,
the child deep inside,
the tree by the river?

In searching through the American poetry of Replansky's era I can find no other American poet who seems so powerfully able to incorporate the lessons of the best surrealist poets. In the 1940s most of us—perhaps I should say "most of the Detroit poets"—didn't even know they existed. Today, for example, the Peruvian poet César Vallejo is accepted as one of the greats of the last century, but still no one other than Replansky has been able to employ his tools without sounding like a parody of the original or a stumbling, foolish imitator. Yet sixty years ago Replansky could do it and sound like no other poet alive writing in English:

> *When there was one kiss*
> *against ten curses*
> *and one loaf*
> *against ten hungry*
> *and one hello*
> *against ten goodbyes*
> *the odds stalked*
> *your crooked steps.*
>
> *And you turned no corner*
> *without heart-tightening*
> *and against ten cannon*
> *you had one fist*
> *and against ten winters*
> *you had one fire.*

Like her masters, Blake and Vallejo, Replansky is an intensely political poet, appalled by the cruelty, greed, and corruption of the masters of nations and corporations, appalled and enraged. I was drawn first to her lyricism, but I soon saw the rightness of her vision, and though I absorbed her vision I was totally incapable of transforming it into poetry. I could with consummate ease rant, and rant. I unfortunately did so in poems or pretend-poems that thankfully no longer exist.

V

By the time I was twenty-one years old I'd begun to think of myself as something of an accomplished poet; what I lacked—among other things—was a recognizable, consistent voice for my poems. For the most part, American poets make this search for a voice automatically—it's part of our native Yankee gift for marketing, this straining after a voice that will make one's poetry sound utterly unlike the work of other poets and hence a unique commodity. It is something like the equivalent—to cite another Detroit effort in the same direction—of adding gigantic tail fins to our cars to make them distinctive. And like the tail fins, it's a mistake. When I read my work loudly enough to myself, it was clear it wasn't prose; that it was not poetry was clear to most everyone else. Fortunately, the voice of my poems was in a constant state of change. Years later I realized that developing a voice before you knew what you needed to say was pointless at best, self-defeating at worst. You could spend years trying to sound as lyrical as Edna St. Vincent Millay or Hart Crane only to discover you wanted to write poetry incendiary enough to burn down General Motors or the Pentagon.

Some of us seemed to find who we were as poets and no doubt as people long before the others. I was not, in this regard, a quick study. One who arrived at both a sense of who he was and his poetic voice—and the absolutely right voice for his particular personality—long before I even knew what a "voice" was or how I would go about finding one or not finding one, was the Miles poet who seemed to me the most innocent as well as the most determined. Paul Petrie had such an original and seemingly natural way of going about his life that one could underestimate the power of his intellect and his emotions. Paul was a tall, spare, athletic man with a shock of dark hair and a very precise way of speaking, and I thought at first he was a recent arrival to Detroit. He seemed too open and friendly to be a native of "my" Detroit, a city not yet dubbed the murder capital of the world but still a place one might regard as threatening. I'd been reading Frost, and so I assumed Paul was a New Englander, probably from Maine, I thought, a man of the earth, weathered and toughened by the earth. When they made the film of Paul, Gary Cooper should play him. But no, he was one of us, raised a few miles from me and educated in the public schools. Compared to Bernard, Paul seemed almost without an ego, and he made not the least effort to project a persona. He was simply who he was, a humble yet confident word-smith. He was also an astute reader of poetry.

We often began our monthly assemblies with one of us presenting the work of a favorite poet or a recent discovery, and it was in the Miles Room that I first encountered Paul. The event was a presentation to a half dozen of us of one of Paul's essential poetic heroes, Elinor Wylie. When he read the following, I thought he might not be serious regarding his admiration:

> *Avoid the reeking herd,*
> *Shun the polluted flock,*
> *Live like that stoic bird,*
> *The eagle of the rock.*

This was actually what inspired him? My God, it was so familiar and clear, I could understand it! Could it be poetry? Bernard went after him: How could he admire such trifles? Why would he read this when he could be reading

Hart Crane? Paul was unflappable. Unlike Bernard's, Paul's tenor voice did not rise an octave when he was challenged. He calmly defended the values of a firm structure, clarity, and good sense, and of a moral center to the best poetry, and then he asked Bernard what was so marvelous about the work of Crane.

Bernard answered with a recitation of the opening of "Repose of Rivers," and claimed that this was the work of a true poet inhabiting the natural world. "'Till age had brought me to the sea,'" answered Paul, quoting from the poem. "Crane died at thirty-two and yet claimed age had brought him to the sea—what a modest chap!"

"At twenty-five Crane knew more than we'll ever know," Bernard said. "What might take one of us a lifetime to 'reach'—in this case an 'inscape,' as Hopkins would say—of the sea, Crane possessed in a trice." (Bernard was astonishingly well read for a teenager and loved to let us know it.)

"Yes, it's a great poem," Petrie said, and then went on to quote the entire poem in a quiet voice 180 degrees from Bernard's operatic style and acknowledge its power and beauty. And quietly added, "By the way, I don't think it's Hart Crane, the poet, boasting that age had brought him to the sea. I think it's the river speaking." How lovely to see Bernard bested for once, and so quietly he barely knew it happened! And wonderful to suddenly realize how complicated this whole poetry thing was and how much room it had for different tastes and personalities, and that the best among us might be the most humble.

It took me ages to realize that the great difference between Paul and Bernard—and me, for that matter—was that Paul wasn't angry at anyone; rage was not his default setting. And even longer to understand that Paul was prodding his poetry toward song and not impassioned speech and for him if his own work lacked melody it wasn't poetry. He seemed so normal and untroubled that for a long time I wondered why he wanted to write poetry at all. This was not, I believed then and believe now, a pose on his part. He was exactly who he seemed to be: a wonderful original who heard music everywhere:

> *The ribald wind unwound my cape*
> *Of thin, alluring, dream-white skin*
> *And left me open to the rape*
> *Of reason's failure, heart's chagrin.*

One late afternoon in our local student hangout whilst he downed a beer—which was one beer more than his usual—he said in all seriousness, "You will be the Keats of our era and I will be the Shelley." He was, of course, wrong on both counts, and a lot more wrong on mine. By the time both he and I graduated—spring of 1950—he into the army and I into Chevy Gear & Axle, Paul was writing well enough to publish in literary journals, and not even several years in the service could dim his focus. I don't know if Paul had read Rilke and believed that childhood was an inexhaustible source of mystery and poetry. Actually he didn't need Rilke or Wordsworth, for that matter, to know the magic of childhood and the dignity of inherited forms:

> *The boys have shaken the cherry tree,*
> *and in the emerald grass*
> *cherries burn like blood in tears of glass.*
>
> *The birds, whose food the cherries were,*
> *desert the shining skies,*
> *and circle the barren earth, and cry.*

Today we might regard Petrie as a postmodernist poet who arrived before the term was invented and drummed to meaninglessness. For someone who seemed so naive he was astonishingly shrewd, perhaps even prescient. In a letter to me written in response to a poem I'd sent him, he asked why there was no humor in my work. I was, he claimed, a genuinely funny person, and he suggested I might try to get my whole self into my writing. At the time I was slightly peeved by the suggestion, perhaps because I was failing to get almost anything of my self into my work.

V I

The Miles Poetry Room subscribed to a number of literary periodicals, several from the UK, and it was in one of these I came upon a poet I'd never heard of whose gumption and directness fascinated me. The work was musical enough, but it did not aim at song but rather at speech, not exactly everyday speech but something that could pass for the usual. At that moment American poetry was carrying on a brief, adulterous affair with Dylan Thomas, who of course was carrying on any number of adulterous affairs; many of our practicing urban poets had suddenly discovered the hayricks in Central Park, the meadows peppered with spotted horses; some heard owls swooping down at night on the Chicago Trade Mart. We seemed hypnotized by his brash lyricism and even brasher behavior. It was thrilling to suddenly awaken to an equally brash poet from England whose work was 180 degrees from Thomas's, work that verged on the "unpoetical": poems that aspired to be hard and factual, at times even brutal, and almost always sounding offhand and reckless.

SIMPLIFY ME WHEN I'M DEAD

Remember me when I'm dead
and simplify me when I'm dead.

As the processes of earth
strip off the colour and the skin:
take the brown hair and blue eye

and leave me simpler than at birth,
when hairless I came howling in
as the moon came in the cold sky.

Of my skeleton perhaps,
so stripped, a learned man will say
"He was of such a type and intelligence," no more.

Thus when in a year collapse
particular memories, you may
deduce, from the long pain I bore

the opinions I held, who was my foe
and what I left, even my appearance
but incidents will be no guide.

Time's wrong-way telescope will show
a minute man ten years hence
and by distance simplified.

Through that lens see if I seem
substance or nothing: of the world
deserving mention, or charitable oblivion,

not by momentary spleen
or love into decision hurled,
leisurely arrive at an opinion.

Remember me when I am dead
and simplify me when I'm dead.

This is a curious poem. In spite of its subject—an imminent death—there is such Olympian calm at the center. A paragraph ago I spoke of its author as "reckless"—yes, I believe that's the right word to describe the way without apology he charges into the matter of his death, and then takes up his finality in such a factual manner you wonder if he's serious. And yes, he is serious, deadly and calmly serious. Does he truly want to be seen "objectively," as the little that's left when his history and even his flesh are stripped away? It would appear so. "See if I seem substance or nothing," he asks, and if nothing, let it be nothing. One could take it as youthful bravado, for the author, Keith Douglas, I read sixty-some years ago in the contributors note, wrote that poem in 1941 when he was twenty-one, exactly my age when first I read the poem. (Poetry has a way of constantly humbling us, its acolytes.) But young as he was, he had to think seriously about life and death, for at the time he was a junior officer in the British army training for service in the Middle East. Within eighteen months he would serve in Palestine, be wounded, hospitalized, return to service, and then take part in the desert warfare in North Africa as a tank commander. That experience would soon find its way into his writing, in a poem that had an enormous impact on my work.

V E R G I S S M E I N N I C H T

Three weeks gone and the combatants gone
returning over the nightmare ground
we found the place again, and found
the soldier sprawling in the sun.

The frowning barrel of his gun
overshadowing. As we came on
that day, he hit my tank with one
like the entry of a demon.

Look. Here in the gunpit spoil
the dishonored picture of his girl
who has put: Steffi. Vergissmeinnicht.
in a copybook gothic script.

We see him almost with content,
abased, and seeming to have paid
and mocked at by his own equipment
that's hard and good when he's decayed.

But she would weep to see today
how on his skin the swart flies move;
the dust upon the paper eye
and the burst stomach like a cave.

For here the lover and killer are mingled
who had one body and one heart.
And death who had the soldier singled
has done the lover mortal hurt.

Let me call this a tough poem, and let me make it clear it is the toughness I admired sixty years ago and still admire, and not the very neat—for me far too neat—conclusion. I can forgive him that, and you might well ask, who the hell am I to forgive Keith Douglas? The answer is no one, a reader and no more. The poem is a bit slipshod, in its phrasing and its rhyming, but it survives whatever weaknesses it possesses because there is pure magic in the details: in the dishonored picture of his girl—yes, his "girl"; in the frowning barrel of his gun; in the copybook gothic script; in that swart fly moving on the skin (perhaps a descendant of the one Emily Dickinson heard buzzing as she died); there is magic in just that dust on the paper eye and in the cave of the burst stomach. After all that precise, frighteningly neutral rendering the poet has a right to poeticize, to speak of the marriage of the killer and the lover and conclude on the rhyme of "one heart" with the hideous "mortal hurt." Pure genius. I was not surprised to discover that Douglas was also a visual artist and often accompanied his poems in his notebooks with drawings.

VII

"Simply reportage," Bernard said in response to my presentation of "Vergissmeinnicht" at the next meeting of the Miles poets. Ruby looked away. Just the least quick little shake of her head told me the poem had affected her but not in any way she welcomed. For perhaps the fifth time Ulysses Wardlaw said after I presented a poem, "Levine, you've got to get into Whitman." Of course Ulysses was absolutely right, and I can't explain why I waited so long to discover our greatest poet; perhaps I simply wasn't ready to absorb a vision as broad, challenging, and profound as Whitman's, perhaps I never would be. Though my age and roughly my height—5'10"—Ulysses had the powerful presence of a great athlete, which he was, as well as a deep, commanding voice. Why didn't I listen more closely to him or to his poetry? For Ulysses had the nerve and craft to do what I'd never then thought of doing: deal with the hard facts of our survival in the industrial Detroit of the heart.

> *Down into the seas of wasted human sweat.*
> *The grind and drive, the meshing of gears,*
> *The dull dead thump, thud of the drop forge*
> *Form, with the hollow ring of steel on steel,*
> *Chains to weight my shoulders and shackle my feet.*

While I was poring over Dylan Thomas and memorizing the loopy sonnets of George Barker, Ulysses was writing my poetry fifteen years before I found the road to it. Whitman may have helped shape the form of his poems, but as a keenly aware black man in post-race-riot Detroit he saw far more clearly than I the limits of Whitman's optimism.

Perhaps that autumn day in 1949 I showed my disappointment for their failure to respond to my discovery. I can remember how I felt but not how I behaved. I know I did not rebuke them, for by that time, at age twenty-one and an aspiring poet for almost eight years, I knew I needed them. Had I known then how quickly I would lose them, how surely they too would join the ranks of "my lost poets," I probably would have reacted differently. I would have been animated by the fear of losing them, and lose them I did. In his early thirties Bernard would die in an auto wreck and leave enough poetry for one tiny, posthumous collection of satiric, hard-edged poems, a collection without any of the dazzling poems of his youth or that singular, naked line, "When in a mirror love redeems my eyes," a line that may live now only in this essay. Ruby would silence her own talent and the powerful sensibility that gave us poetry. She who once lived so vibrantly in verse and could write so openly, "Today/ I gave my cheek to snow / that didn't want to die / the common death" and "The bread I eat and call my own / Is coarse, cross-grained, born / Of an old woman's sighs and groans. / It sleeps within me like a stone": within five years she would be driven by the need to ease the suffering of others, and so take her talent and herself into the wilderness of Latin America and vanish. Unappreciated, unpublished, out of sync with the America of the 1950s, the America of Jim Crow, *The Ed Sullivan Show,* Elvis, and the politics of HUAC and Joseph McCarthy, Ulysses Wardlaw would be silenced. All his youthful idealism and lyrical belief in our country would suffocate.

Back then I didn't know just how much I needed them or how much they'd already given me. I needed not merely their encouragement, their criticism, their intelligence and dedication and their soulfulness—for these were powerfully soulful people—and their fellowship in our ancient discipline. I think more than anything I needed their belief that we would share in the singular glory of poetry. Where would I have been without that belief, without Bernard, Ruby, Paul, and Ulysses, my comrades whose words inspired me, whose belief in me kept me going? Where would I have been without all of them, without Capetanakis and his strange vision of our origins, without Alun Lewis and the songs he hurled in death's face, without Replansky and her righteous indignation, her struggle to resurrect the true Americas of William Blake and César Vallejo, without the calm and surgical poems of Keith Douglas, without the dreams of all my lost or forgotten poets, my brothers and sisters in madness and glory who shared with me their faith in the power of the perfect words, the words we knew as children and then forgot?

NOBODY'S DETROIT

I left Detroit in 1954. I was twenty-six years old and had a BA in English. I left a job I liked, "driving truck"—as they said then—for a company that repaired electric motors of all sizes. The job got me out in the fresh air—if you can call the air in a manufacturing town fresh—and it took me to the little machine shops, the small-parts makers, the tool-and-die outfits we serviced on the worst days to that empire of arrogance and monumental ugliness Ford River Rouge, then the largest industrial complex in the world. The year before that I'd worked for Railway Express, delivering trunks and parcels to the four corners of the town, so I knew the geography and the neighborhoods of the place. It was my city and I hated leaving: it was home to my family and all my best friends, it was home to the little circle of poets I'd become a part of; its tree-lined streets and its street life, its humble houses, its libraries, theaters, jazz clubs, its birds, beasts, and flowers, and especially its people had nourished me and would as the years passed not only enter my writing—at times they would command it. So why did I leave? Let's just say it was for love, not money.

Twenty-eight years later I was invited back to read at the retirement party of one of my favorite English teachers at Wayne University (which in the meantime had become Wayne State). I was to be the surprise guest, a major player in the event. It was a short flight from Boston, where I was then living, and when the plane landed I looked for my appointed driver. There was a young and attractive woman bearing a sign with my name on it. No, she was not taking me into town; she was from Delta Air Lines and had a sealed envelope for me. Inside was a note from the chair of the English department and in the note instructions for getting into town by bus and also a badly drawn map showing me where to appear that afternoon for the planned *hommage*. It seemed I honored my old school more than it honored me. Since Jay, my teacher, had no idea I was coming, I decided I would skip the catered meal and show up at the last possible moment, give my talk, read a poem, embrace my old mentor, and then escape. Hopefully my absence until the crucial moment would cost the chair as much anxiety as possible.

I had hours to kill. Coming in on the west side of town, I got off the bus near the ballpark. Alas, the season had ended and that year there was no postseason for the Tigers. Half a mile south of the stadium the plumbing-parts factory where I'd worked for a year was gone, and nothing was in its place except a field of nettles and weeds and three abandoned cars, their wheels gone. I walked farther south, toward the river, and to my astonishment I found a large fenced-in garden—tomatoes, corn, squash, and rows of exquisite zinnias, all those things I'd tried unsuccessfully to grow in my victory garden during World War II. The gardener appeared from nowhere and asked me if I wanted a closer look. He opened the gate—which hadn't been locked—and took me down the rows, named the various crops while boasting only the least bit about the perfection of his tomatoes ("so good they remind you what tomatoes taste like"), and finally showed me the area he'd reserved for his winter crop. No, he didn't have permission from the city; these days no one asked the city for anything. There'd once been a nice two-story house on this ground, but it was gone, just got up and left, and then the land was empty, so why not use it? The fence was here to keep the dogs out; it was like the

Depression years—which we both recalled—with packs of wild dogs cut loose by their owners and left to their own devices, foraging and wandering, "That's what we all do to survive here," he said. The day had grown unseasonably warm, and so we removed ourselves to the shade of his front porch across the street. How he guessed I was from Detroit, I don't know, but he did, and he was curious to know when I'd left and why I'd come back. When I told him I was here to celebrate the retirement of my old teacher, he rocked back and forth a moment and said, "That's beautiful, that is biblical." There are those rare times in my life when I know that what I'm living is in a poem I've still to write. As we sat in silence, I took in as much of the scene as I could until my eyes were filled with so much seeing I finally had to close them.

> *On this block seven houses*
>   *are still here to be counted,*
> *and if you count the shacks*
>   *housing illegal chickens,*
> *the pens for dogs, the tiny*
>   *pig sty that is half cave . . .*
> *and if you count them you can*
>   *count the crows' nest*
> *in the high beech tree*
>   *at the corner, and you can*
> *regard the beech tree itself*
>   *bronzing in mid-morning light*
> *as the mast of the great ship*
>   *sailing us all back*
> *into the 16th century*
>   *or into the present age's*
> *final discovery . . .*

My guide for that morning was named Tom; I gave him the surname of Jefferson and put him in the poem "A Walk with Tom Jefferson." I left out a remark he made that seemed to encapsulate his vision of our city. After he catalogued the disappearance of all but the seven houses that remained on the block, for want of something better to say, I remarked, "Nothing lasts forever." He turned his weathered face to me and amended my judgment: "Nothing lasts." If you grew up in Detroit when Tom and I grew up, that could easily become the mantra for your city and your life: "Nothing lasts."

That was neither the first nor the last time I returned to the city, but it was probably the most memorable, and in retrospect it was the last time I felt truly at home there. Of course that was due to the character of this aging black man, a retired auto worker, who'd welcomed me back. Before I took off for the English department ceremony, I remarked to Tom that many people regarded me as a deserter for leaving Detroit for another life. He advised me to ignore such responses, they were petty and rose out of jealousy, and he added, "All the smart ones left." What that return had in common with all the others was a mounting sense of change, and seldom change for the better. Some things had improved. Wayne State had come up in the world with a new library and a clean and extended campus. There was less traffic on Woodward Avenue (no doubt because there was less reason to be there). The Fisher Theater was restored. There was eventually a new baseball park. When I was invited back several years ago to read my poetry, I was assured things were improving, but when I got there my eyes told me otherwise.

The Italian poet Giuseppe Ungaretti wrote of his native city, Alexandria, "My city destroys and annihilates itself from instant to instant." He'd left in 1912, when he was a young, aspiring writer, but he carried the place with him for the rest of his life. For him it was already an ancient and mythic city, a great port risen out of a desert and founded long before its classic naming. Curiously, even in his imagination the city revised itself, and for the rest of his life he relived his childhood and young manhood in an Alexandria that had transformed itself into something fabulous and dreamlike:

> *I saw you, Alexandria,*
> *Crumbling on your spectral foundation*
> *Becoming for me a memory*
> *In a spectral embrace of lights.*

He wrote those lines after a short visit home twenty years after his initial departure. By then the modern era was well under way with its indifference to the geography of home. I've wondered if even in 1932, when he returned, he was able to see the city that was there, or had it been so powerfully displaced by the visionary city of his imagination that the hard facts meant nothing? In a poem written near the end of his life, he gives us a wild, hallucinatory vision of the city as it was on the day of his own birth:

> *There was a squall, it rained heavily*
> *At Alexandria in Egypt on that night . . .*
> *A child galloped on a white horse*
> *And around him in a throng the people*
> *Clung together in the circle of the soothsayers . . .*

Quite suddenly in the poem his mother appears, an actual person, "a Lucchese," no less (she was born in Lucca); she laughs and quotes an old peasant proverb: *"If the lanes run in February, / it fills all one's crocks with oil and wine."* The mother recites one of her bits of "folk wisdom" her son has never taken seriously, and the nightmare spell is broken. The transformation comes about not by any magic or special incantation, but by a common saying in a common language. Now the poet is back in the constant flux of creation, or, to quote García Lorca, he has become witness to "the unending baptism of newly created things."

When Ungaretti wrote those lines, he was almost as old as I am now. (He lived to be eighty-two.) He never again returned to Alexandria, but with some luck I'll get back to Detroit, if you can call that luck. What will I find? I know the house on Pingree, the house of my earliest memories, is gone: that is, it's not a house anymore. I saw it in a film of the town taken forty years after the great rebellion of 1967 (labeled "riots" by the newspapers). It had been pared down to brickwork, a flight of steps, and a blackened chimney. Each time I replayed the film it reappeared, a silhouette in black and white. It had become something historical, an anonymous ruin left by one of the century's wars, something akin to the dwelling immortalized in the poem "Five Minutes After the Air Raid" by the great Czech poet Miroslav Holub:

> *she climbed to the third floor*
> *up stairs which were all that was left*
> *of the whole house,*
> *she opened the door*
> *full on to the sky,*
> *stood gaping over the edge.*
>
> *For this was the place*
> *the world ended.*

Even if I looked for either of the two General Motors plants I worked in, I wouldn't find it; they've both been torn down. The Mavis Nu-Icy-Bottling Company, where at sixteen I earned a dollar an hour, was flattened and carted off, though I found the railroad spur that led to the loading dock. The home of Dolly Basil, whom I truly loved for two months, has given way to a six-lane highway. For certain I won't find the little scenes of childhood I've carried in amber all these years like amulets against the inevitable, the images that once told me who I was and that now belong in someone else's biography, or no one's.

•

I learned recently that after the fire of 1805, Detroit adopted the motto "Speramus meliora; resurget cineribu": We hope for better things; it will arise from the ashes. I discovered this motto in a statement by the photographer Andrew Moore; in the same statement he described a school warehouse the roof of which had collapsed, allowing a grove of birch trees to sprout from "a dense matting of decayed and burned books." Everything we Detroiters created self-destructs, while the trees—rising from "the richly rotting words"— head straight skyward. I like to imagine the delicate leaves of those birch trees, each one bearing a poem to the heavens, an original poem, wise and stoic, from a sensibility that has seen it all. The poems would have to be brief and precise—you can't get that much on a leaf—but they would also have to say perfectly all they've learned.

From Moore's astonishing photographs I discovered much more—and not about a distant past but about the present and the future. The city that I thought had nowhere to go and hence had stopped changing, that I believed had stepped out of history and simply begun to disappear one block at a time while no one noticed, has been caught in Moore's work in the small daily acts of disguise and revision. And while it may seem ridiculous to say, the photographs document a new growth. In one photograph, a door opens into an empty room in an abandoned building, a room in the act of acquiring a new floor, this one vivid and green, perhaps composed of mold, perhaps of something never seen before. In another, a young woman comes to the back door of her house; she holds it ajar and looks out impassively at the world. Five steps lead down to a concrete walkway; she doesn't take them. A hundred and fifty square feet, more or less, of siding have vanished from the back wall of the house, and someone has splashed patches of color—red, blue, orange, yellow, peach—on the otherwise naked board, perhaps the same person who neatly painted a blue vertical stripe on the green door. The overturned red bathtub, the wrecked pram whose motto is "carsick," what do they tell us about the mistress of the house? One hand on the doorknob, the other on the doorjamb, she stands firmly in place, knees slightly bent, just in case. Don't mess with her! At the very bottom of the picture, and hence closest to the photographer, there are tiny patches of bright grass and clover growing out of a dense soil. The world doesn't quit.

•

When I recall Chevy Gear & Axle or Detroit Transmission—the two GM plants I worked in—I don't see color; I see both interiors in the same black-and-white movie that captured the old house on Pingree. In Moore's industrial photographs there is both color and texture: the browns and pebbled grays of the brick walls, the subtle and lovely blues of painted and aged steel. And much to my surprise, light—a soft golden light—breaking through the upper windows. (How can I have forgotten that light? And now it comes to me: I worked nights in both places. At the end of each shift I would see the windows slowly gray and know I'd made it. Golden light I never saw.) In one magnificent horizontal view of a huge abandoned space we see an intricate spider web of steel speeding toward the horizon, where a rectangle of pure light waits at the farthest end of the factory. This sudden revelation of sublimity in a place I can only think of as a hellhole simply stops me. I know I never saw anything like this, probably because I wasn't seeing.

In some of Moore's photographs I don't know what I'm looking at. In a gray, vertical, industrial interior something as milky as a waterfall drops from a loft to a floor heaped with plastic garbage only to become part of a tentlike shelter in which a small fire burns. Someone is inside that shelter, someone built it, someone found the little table and placed it precisely there, someone arranged all the items just as they are, someone may regard it as home; he or she might be drying clothes on a line, or perhaps they're just rags. The only color in this picture—except for a few scraps of red plastic in the junk pile—comes from the intense yellow flame, which dyes the shelter's interior a warm magenta. Through the dust of the upper windows a dirty light settles on the scene. No, it's not the setting for a "dreadful martyrdom" out of Brueghel, where—to use Auden's language—"the torturer's horse / Scratches its innocent behind on a tree," but some strange rite is acting itself out before my eyes; what it is I don't know. But it is Detroit, so it must have something to do with survival.

There are very few people in these photographs: someone's leg shows in that tentlike shelter; there is the impassive woman at her back door; in another picture inside a ruined building a man holding a thick pipe stands on a truck bed—he is expressionless. In another, however, I can see one man half-smiling as he sits beside the driver of a tiny truck negotiating a factory in Highland Park—perhaps the old Ford plant, for the little truck bears the signature of "Ford" in the familiar script. And finally there are four children and one person large enough to be an adult standing in the middle of an empty road that leads nowhere; the three larger children are dressed alike, white shirts and dark blue trousers—no doubt a school uniform—and carry backpacks. Their young faces give away nothing. Those were the only people I found in over three dozen pictures, but our work and our words are evident everywhere in Moore's Detroit. As for our work, perhaps the less said the better. Gazing into the windows of Cass Tech—once the finest high school in the city—all I can see is debris; the building itself looks substantial from the outside, but the windows have been removed, and what's been done to each classroom would suggest that the last class of students so hated their time at Cass they took revenge upon the desks, the shelves, the books, the tables, the lights, the chairs, even the walls. "Wiser not to ask just what has occurred," Auden wrote in the mid-1930s about sudden alarming changes that could be omens of even more alarming changes.

And we who civilized the place have left our words, little found poems that might better have been lost. At the intersection of Brush Street and something, a strange mist obscures the wreckage of a house. In an elegant handwriting someone has written "away" on a curious brown faux tree trunk beside the street sign. On the street sign the city says "Brush," and the people's representative answers "away."

In an unidentified interior going to ruin a wall clock has stopped telling time. The face of the clock is peeling away; we still have "5," "6," "7," "8" in good shape, a tiny portion of "4," but up above, both "11" and "12" are sliding down into nonsense. If we didn't get the point, the clockmaker's name and logo survive: "NATIONAL TIME." All three hands are still here, but they appear to be frozen in "NATIONAL TIME." In another photograph a field of weeds and wild grasses is crowned with a squat reddish-brown tank proudly announcing its ownership: FUEL OIL CORP. Eight of the eleven letters, not chosen at random, are repeated upside-down in the puddles that have formed in the eroding road that runs past. Above looms an English sky borrowed from a nineteenth-century painting by Constable. When you get close to the tank it appears to have been embellished with a covering of wooden slats now rotting away—that have no function except to beautify what cannot be beautiful. In the photograph titled *Police Desk* we discover in the chaos of a junked office several large poster-sized sheets with the intriguing titles "Debbie Friday," "Vickie Truelove," "Monterey Motel," and "Valerie Chalk." "Debbie Friday" is the only one that reveals more than its title. It shows two drawings of a head, one from the front, one from the back. Down below the drawings there is a small rectangular box that reads:

HEIGHT = 5'5"
WEIGHT = 153 LBS.

There's one more found poem in the same picture, one not worth repeating, and so it is repeated in ghostlike letters in the cinderblocks that compose a bared wall, sometimes in whole, sometimes in part:

FIRE

MICH-GYPSUM-CO

PROOF

The most eloquent of all the found poems adorns another picture; it's written in gilt in old English script on the railing of the second deck of the blasted interior of what looks like a once proud house of worship:

AND YOU SHALL SAY GOD DID IT

(The initial quotation mark has surrendered half of itself. The church has surrendered a good deal more.) I expect the inscription was placed there in better times and had no reference to the destruction that now greets the eye; but if it was true regarding all that the parishioners once celebrated, it just might be true now. The photograph would appear to think so even if the parishioners wouldn't.

In his famous photo of a roadside stand shot in Birmingham, Alabama, in 1936—an equally tough time—Walker Evans chose cozier, less ironic phrases:

F.M. POINTER

THE OLD RELIABLE

HOUSE MOVER

FISH AND LAKE FISH

HONEST WEIGHTS, SQUARE DEALINGS

Below the motto is a painting of a very plump fish to whet the appetite. Somewhere in Alabama in '36 he took a picture of a boarding house in good repair bearing this sign:

MORRIS HOTEL
ROOMS .50 AND UP
ROOM AND BOARD $30.00

Things in small-town USA back then would seem to have been possible, if not exactly inviting. I've stayed in worse-looking digs. There is a solidity and sureness in Evans's Depression photos; the two-story frame houses of Bethlehem, Pennsylvania, are dwarfed by the mills, but they are upright and serviceable, they march up and down the hills in unison and defy the smog and the weather. The little found poems in Evans—often illustrated—seem so friendly by comparison to Moore's. In Tuscaloosa in 1935 Evans found an antebellum house of considerable grandeur but no longer a house; it was transformed into the home of TUSCALOOSA WRECKING CO., which may be quite a comedown for so stately a place, but at least it's retained its usefulness. By contrast, in Moore's photographs what were once homes or workplaces or houses of worship have collapsed into chaos or pure design, or in some cases they've been swallowed up by a carnivorous conspiracy of trees, shrubs, moss, ice, exhaustion. In his world we learn that even the grandest constructions and the hardest objects can give up their shapes and purposes. Nothing stays the same.

What we see taking place in Andrew Moore's photographs is no doubt happening everywhere, but it would appear that in Detroit the process has such extraordinary velocity it seems to have stepped out of time to become the sole condition of being. These photographs are among the most beautiful I've ever seen: their calm in the face of the ravages of man and nature confer an unexpected dignity upon the subjects of his camera, the very dignity I had assumed daily life had robbed them of. In an untitled photograph my eye settles on a small sheet of ice that has formed in a wheelbarrow and moves from the ice to the portions of the twigs sticking up though trapped in the ice, and then from the twigs to the barrow's single visible handle and then to the black trunk of a tree that snakes its way upward through the half-light trapped between two buildings. The trunk continues upward toward . . . toward what it doesn't know, and yet it continues to rise. This dignity of the isolated and inconsequential, of all that refuses to not be, I originally encountered as a teenage aspiring poet in that most American of writers, William Carlos Williams, but in Williams it was in a great poem of birth, "Spring and All":

> *All along the road the reddish*
> *purplish, forked, upstanding, twiggy*
> *stuff of bushes and small trees*
> *with dead, brown leaves under them*
> *leafless vines—*
>
> *Lifeless in appearance, sluggish*
> *dazed spring approaches—*
>
> *They enter the new world naked,*
> *cold, uncertain of all*
> *save that they enter . . .*

Like Williams's poems in *Spring and All*, Andrew Moore's photographs honor what is most ignored and despised among us, and they do so in such a straightforward manner that unless we're attentive we can miss the art. When I write that these pictures are a revelation, I've not begun to describe their effect on me, nor have I begun to describe the profundity of the debt I owe them. I had thought my city no longer mattered, that I—as one of its poets—had been writing for sixty-five years about next to nothing, that my life's work was only a footnote to the history of American idiocy and hubris. I had thought I knew what it meant to be from Detroit, to be of Detroit, to be Detroit. In truth I didn't know the half of it.

ON FINDING
WILLIAM CARLOS WILLIAMS
AND MY POETRY

The first anthology that introduced me to modern poetry was *A Little Treasury of Modern Poetry,* edited by Oscar Williams. Why such a book should have seven times as many poems by Oscar Williams as by W. C. Williams did not then puzzle or amuse me. (Even today it's a wonderful, though dated, anthology as well as a testament to the immense ego of one less-than-mediocre poet, its editor.) I was eighteen, the age at which one simply devours books whole. Within a few weeks I fell under the sway of T. S. Eliot and W. H. Auden with that enthusiasm that first discovery brings. I was just beginning my second career as writer of what I hoped would be poetry, the first having ended when I was sixteen and discovered the allure of women—or girls, as we then called them. By the age of twenty I had discovered Gerard Manley Hopkins and Hart Crane, initially through the same anthology, and then there burst upon the American scene that extraordinary Welshman Dylan Thomas. I heard him read in Detroit when I was twenty-two, and I truly couldn't get enough of him; he alerted me to a number of poets by presenting them at this reading: Edward Thomas and Thomas Hardy and, among Americans, John Crowe Ransom and Theodore Roethke. Shortly thereafter I journeyed to New York City to hear Thomas at the 92nd Street Y, and I carried with me a letter of introduction from one of my mentors in Detroit to Oscar Williams, who had promised to introduce me to Dylan Thomas after the reading.

Something extraordinary in my life as a poet that had nothing to do with Thomas or his reading happened that night. When I entered the auditorium it was crowded and I couldn't find Oscar, but I did catch sight of John Malcolm Brinnin, who was then managing the poetry series at the Y. I asked in my most authoritative voice if Brinnin had seen "the poet Williams." Brinnin's reply was the event: "Do you mean Oscar or the great Williams?" The great Williams, alas, was not in attendance. More to the point, I had almost no experience with his work, nor any idea how much I was missing. Oscar was there and through him I met Thomas, who treated me with courtesy and tact. We exchanged a few banalities, and then he went off with a beautiful woman a head taller than he.

Curiously enough, it was through the writing of the poet-critic Yvor Winters that I first discovered the validity of Brinnin's remark. I have no idea now what Winters wrote, but he did quote Williams's poem "Spring and All." Everything else in Winters's truly remarkable volume of criticism *In Defense of Reason* faded for that moment into the background, for I knew without the slightest doubt that I was reading a great poem, one of the greatest poems ever written in my country and in the spoken language of my country, a poem written by a living American. Until that reading, my models had been Crane, Eliot, Auden, Yeats, Hardy, and Dylan Thomas, but what I was reading cast them all into the shadows—not for others, perhaps, but certainly for me. I knew my future was somehow through this poet. I must have read the poem a hundred times in the next few months, and I would feel passages of it welling up inside me like totems against all the claims of the smallness of our poetry.

I began publishing my own work in journals in the

spring of '54, and in one of the first magazines in which I appeared, a thin and stapled-together issue of *Poetry*, was a section of one of Williams's great later poems, "Asphodel, That Greeny Flower." My own poem on that occasion was formal, rhymed pentameter, and, while the diction and syntax struggled to echo speech, beside the magnificent ease of the Williams I sounded stuffy and far more rational and reserved than I actually am. I was struck by the fact that in some strange way Williams sounded more like me than I did—that is, more like me if only I were wise, masterful, and a genius. At the time, recently married a second time, I was living completely apart from the world of poetry in Tallahassee, Florida, where my wife taught at the local college while I finished my MA thesis for Wayne University on the odes of Keats. And I wrote poetry and taught myself what I could. I had had one great writing teacher, John Berryman, at the University of Iowa writing program, and to some degree I had internalized his insights into my work.

The next year I returned to Iowa to teach technical writing and "The Bible as Literature," which required my reading of the New Testament. This was my first university teaching experience, and I found it exhausting. At the time I often wondered how those giants Stevens and Williams held down full-time positions, one in commerce, the other in medicine, and still wrote so much and at such a level of intensity. I attended Paul Engle's workshops and got very little from them; but my best poet friends there— Paul Petrie, Henri Coulette, and Peter Everwine, then all formalists—were readers I could trust and from whom I learned. I don't believe that at that time they shared my secret passion for Williams. In '57 I attended Stanford on a fellowship to study with Yvor Winters, who—to my profound disappointment—had lost much of his enthusiasm

for Williams. He was extremely kind to me, and spent a
good deal of time introducing me to some of his favorite
poets—he had only two students in his writing seminar, and
so there was ample time for private sessions. Three of those
poets impressed me hugely: Ben Jonson, Tristan Corbière,
and Elizabeth Daryush. I had been writing mainly formalist
work for Winters, but the moment I read Daryush, I felt I'd
discovered an incredible poetic source. I began to imitate
her syllabic experiments, which I found astonishing, for
working from her models allowed me both to possess for-
mal requirements and to use a diction as close to speech as
possible while keeping a measure of control, or perhaps—to
employ Williams's own vocabulary—a control of the mea-
sure. Her work was difficult to locate at that time—it may
still be—but in the rare book room of the Stanford library
was a gorgeously printed version of her collected poems
that I, with clean hands and a pencil, was allowed to pore
over and copy. Her subject matter rarely interested me,
so there was little chance of my being held captive by her
poetry the way I'd been by the writing of Dylan Thomas
ten years earlier. But I loved the quiet unobtrusiveness of
her rhymed syllabics, which allowed that voice so close to
speech it sounded like speech but more precise and elegant.

Corbière influenced me in another way, in terms of
what the poet wrote about—the maimed, the isolated, the
despised—but that influence would not enter my work for
some years, because at that time I simply lacked the craft to
reach into such lives with any authority. It was at this point
in my writing life that the full force of Williams's poetry hit
me; I suddenly realized that I could incorporate much of
what I loved in his work and be simply free, a condition my
chaotic life seemed unable to tolerate.

Looking back at what I then wrote—the best of which

is in my first book, *On the Edge*—I can easily see that I was suddenly writing for the first time, and for better or worse, poems that are recognizably mine. What in poetry we call "voice" had arrived. In truth I hadn't been looking for it; I'd been trying as best I could to cope with the demands of putting words down that made sense and had rhythm and resonance while somehow reflecting both my experience as a person with my particular past and my feelings toward those events. I can hear underneath every happy moment in the writing the influence—subtle, I hope—of the greatest American poet of my century.

I'm seventy-six now, so most of my writing is behind me. As I hear my own poetry in spite of the many changes in it over the years, I still catch the echo of the rhythms of my master Williams. Since my early thirties I've largely made my living teaching, first literature and composition and later poetry writing. At my age it would make sense to retire altogether, but I find enormous stimulation in teaching a class a year, and I seem to catch some of the enthusiasm and wonder for poetry I find in the best beginning poets. If I hold up, I'll be teaching this fall, and I know that once again I'll present one poem for certain to my class, "Spring and All," and I'll try to make the poets understand why it was the most important poem I ever read and how it turned me away from my English masters toward the effort to create a poetry original and audacious enough to be American.

DETROIT JAZZ
IN THE LATE FORTIES
AND EARLY FIFTIES

I REMEMBER CLIFFORD

Wakening in a small room,
the walls high and blue, one high window
through which the morning enters,
I turn to the table beside me
painted a thick white. There instead
of a clock is a tumbler of water,
clear and cold, that wasn't there
last night. Someone quietly entered,
and now I see the white door
slightly ajar and around three sides
the light on fire. I remember once
twenty-seven years ago walking
the darkened streets
of my home town when up ahead
on Joy Road at the Blue Bird of Happiness
I heard over the rumble of my own head
for the first time the high clear trumpet
of Clifford Brown calling us all
to the dance he shared with us
such a short time. My heart quickened
and in my long coat, breathless
and stumbling, I ran
through the swirling snow
to the familiar sequined door
knowing it would open on something new.

•

The title "I Remember Clifford" comes from a fabulous melody written by the saxophonist Benny Golson as a tribute to his departed friend the astonishingly gifted jazz trumpeter Clifford Brown, who died at age twenty-five in an auto accident. Where do talents such as Brown's come from—and how do we come to deserve such gifts? The poem is concerned with the sudden generosity of the world, the unexplainable giving that occurs in the midst of deprivation, for I discovered the moment of Clifford deep in the misery of one of the hardest years of my life. A door opened, and this music—unexpected and unearned by me—was suddenly mine, pure, free, clear, as water was in my early years. Yes, I'm trying to say that music like water is essential to life, for in fact I can't imagine a life without music.

Do I truly remember Clifford? I honestly don't know, for this was almost fifty years ago. I am simply not sure I ever saw him at the Blue Bird, but every time I hear that tune I think of the Blue Bird and the excitement of going to that place. (It may be that the trumpet I actually heard that night was that of Thad Jones.) The place was a big rectangular café with a bar on your left as you entered and the bandstand on your immediate right, with maybe a dozen tables facing it. The place was unusually well behaved—the owner, who was reputed to have served time for murder, kept the patrons subdued. My favorite among the "regulars" was the young alto man Eddie Jamison (who inspired a section of my poem "The Angels of Detroit," though my guess is the events recorded in the poem have nothing to do with fact); Jamison's style was based on Bird's, and Charlie Parker was then my favorite musician. The other regulars included Art Mardigan on drums, Phil Hill on piano, and Abe Woodly on vibes.

The Blue Bird was home for me on Friday nights. I remember Thad Jones playing there often; his power and delicacy were not to be forgotten. Billy Mitchell was also there a lot—a big, full tenor sound; he played with great energy and fire. Frank Foster, another great tenor. And when Wardell Gray was present, he brought a special excitement to the place. (I later learned that Miles Davis played there for some months during the fall and winter of '51, but all that year I was working afternoons—four p.m. to midnight—and was too worn out even for music.)

•

I had the good luck to discover Pres early, at age eighteen. In my first semester at Wayne, then the city university of Detroit, I was seated in an English class next to a big Irish brawler whose passion was Lester Young, whom I had never heard of. My new friend so loved the music of Pres he arranged a dance at his old high school and talked them into inviting Pres to play. A couple hundred kids, mainly white, showed up for the event—held on a Saturday night, and staged in the gym. My friend and I watched from the track, which served as the balcony that night; this was the autumn of '46, and Pres was breathtaking. Of course almost no one danced. We were too mesmerized to even move.

Eight years later I saw him again in Detroit, playing at a toilet on Grand River not far from where my grandfather had his used-car-parts grease shop. That night it seemed as though everything had abandoned Pres except his horn. When he wanted to, he could revive the real Lester Young from memory, playing some of the great old pieces brilliantly, though at any moment he might stop playing and do some graceless dance on the bandstand. During the second set he lost control, demanded to be paid on the spot, and would not listen to the young Detroit trumpet man who begged him to behave. Except for one drunk in the place, the audience was listening—we knew he was Pres—but this jerk had come up to the bandstand and insisted on "directing" the musicians. Lester didn't seem in the least bothered by the man and let the guy carry on, though the other members of the band were clearly distracted or worse. And quite suddenly Lester exploded, not at this fool but at the owner of the place, who was tending bar. A shouting match ensued; Lester was demanding to be paid for something else he'd done that day—as I recall, it was a radio appearance for some deejay—and the owner claimed he'd had nothing to do with that. Finally the exasperated owner paid him off, and Lester stomped off into the night while the young band members packed up. I was reminded of seeing Zero Mostel, down on his luck, in a cheap nightclub in Miami Beach during the summer of '49. A woman in the audience began to heckle him—he was doing a stand-up routine and getting no laughs—and he suddenly pulled down his pants, revealing long, flowered boxer shorts. He grabbed his crotch and shouted to the woman, "You don't even deserve this!"

ONE WORD

Western High School gym, Friday night dance,
spring of '47. Lester Young
playing for the edification
of two hundred mainly white teenagers

four of whom are off dancing in a corner.
Up on the indoor track my buddy Conway,
the Irish brawler and hockey player,
who organized the entire evening,
turns to me and says a single word
that justifies his rapture, his hard eyes
watering: "Pres." By which he means Lester
is the president not only of
the greatest tenor sax of the world and
of our hearts, he means Lester has made
it back from eight months in an army stockade
for merely being who he is, from
what we two, being kids, have no words for.

The years were there to teach us. Conway
would battle his father for the old house
in Del Ray and win only to lose out
to the bank. He'd get his first real kill
in the air over Korea. I would find
him in '59, drunk in a white bar
on Second Avenue, an Air Force Major,
ready to fight even me. Lester
would return from Paris that year, alone,
to die in New York of malnutrition
and the need not to live. If I close
my eyes I can still hear him come in late
on "Easy Living" and sail out just
behind the beat, lightly, to sing and sing
until Conway turns to me his eyes filled
with all he must learn and says the one word.

•

Early fifties, in one of the less grand downtown picture palaces, I heard Billie Holiday for the first and only time. I was seated high in the second balcony and looking almost straight down on Billie and her pianist. The stage dark except for the spots on the two of them. The theater completely sold out; everyone let out a breath when she came on stage. Billie in a white dress, her hair adorned with a white gardenia. I was stunned by her physical beauty and grace; I'd heard so much about her difficulties and addictions I was not prepared for such a powerful woman. For years I'd listened to those early records with Teddy Wilson, Lester, Chu Berry, Benny Goodman, so I was not expecting this huskier, deeper voice. She'd lost that floating quality that had delighted me with its lyric understatement and ease. The new power was different: frank, pained, and unrelenting. She was a different singer, probably a different woman, and still the greatest jazz singer ever. I was surprised by the perfect clarity of her articulation: above all else it was the songs she presented. She ended with "Strange Fruit" and brought the house down, but I liked best "Foolin' Myself," "Easy Living," "Mean to Me," and "I Must Have That Man," the songs I knew so well, sung with an unexpected authority. Almost thirty years later, home after a difficult and lonely journey of some months, I played "Easy Living," and that night years earlier in Detroit came back to me with undeniable force.

•

SONGS

Dawn coming in over the fields
of darkness takes me by surprise

and I look up from my solitary road
pleased not to be alone, the birds
now choiring from the orange groves
huddling to the low hills. But sorry
that this night has ended, a night
in which you spoke of how little love
we seemed to have known and all of it
going from one of us to the other.
You could tell the words took me
by surprise, as they often will, and you
grew shy and held me away for a while,
your eyes enormous in the darkness,
almost as large as your hunger
to see and be seen over and over.

30 years ago I heard a woman sing
of the motherless child sometimes
she felt like. In a white dress
this black woman with a gardenia
in her hair leaned on the piano
and stared out into the breathing darkness
of unknown men and women needing
her songs. There were those among
us who cried, those who rejoiced
that she was back before us for a time,
a time not to be much longer, for
the voice was going and the habits
slowly becoming all there was of her.

And I believe that night she cared
for the purity of the songs and not
much else. Oh, she still saw
the slow gathering of that red dusk
that hovered over her cities, and no

doubt dawns like this one caught
her on the roads from job to job,
but the words she'd lived by were
drained of mystery as this sky
is now, and there was no more "Easy
Living" and she was "Miss Brown" to
no one and no one was her "Lover Man."
The only songs that mattered were wordless
like those rising in confusion from
the trees or wind-songs that waken
the grass that slept a century, that
waken me to how far we've come.

•

Went one spring to the Paradise Theater on Woodward Avenue—the main drag of Detroit—to see Art Tatum and instead got Erroll Garner. A guy came out on the stage to announce that Tatum's flight was delayed, but he was going to make it, and until he did we would have Garner playing without bass or drums. With short breaks Garner went on bravely for what seemed like several hours. I confess it felt like a lot of Garner. Finally, after eleven p.m., the great man arrived with a bassist and a drummer. They got right into it after Tatum thanked the audience for staying—I would guess more than half of us had declined the offer of a refund and stayed to hear him play nonstop for hours. The next evening, near the Flame Show Bar, on John R, I saw Tatum and the bass player. I crossed the street intending to thank him; I was also curious to know what a genius would talk about: I suspected it would be a discussion of the works of Darius Milhaud or Stravinsky. What I actually heard I recorded in the poem "On the Corner."

ON THE CORNER

Standing on the corner
until Tatum passed
blind as the sea,
heavy, tottering
on the arm of the young
bass player, and they
both talking
Jackie Robinson.
It was cold, late,
and the Flame Show Bar
was crashing
for the night, even
Johnny Ray
calling it quits.
Tatum said, Can't
believe how fast
he is to first. Wait'll
you see Mays
the bass player said.
Women in white furs
spilled out of the bars
and trickled toward
the parking lot. Now
it could rain, coming
straight down. The man
in the brown hat
never turned his head up.
The gutters swirled
their heavy waters,
the streets reflected

the sky, which was
nothing. Tatum
stamped on toward
the Bland Hotel, a wet
newspaper stuck
to his shoe, his mouth
open, his vest
drawn and darkening.
I can't hardly wait, he said.

It took me years to realize how beautiful was the modesty of Erroll Garner that night at the Paradise. He knew the audience had come to hear Tatum, he certainly knew—as a gifted musician—how great a difference there was between his command and Tatum's; yet he did his best. I didn't then appreciate how heroic Garner was; I hadn't yet learned that the world is overpopulated with people who never tire of hearing themselves. I was only just starting to meet other poets.

•

Saw Bird in an intimate setting in Detroit only once. (First saw the legend with Jazz at the Philharmonic at Masonic Temple, but those evenings were dominated by Illinois Jacquet playing "How High the Moon" with such fervor and showmanship he got us all to screaming.) At the Flame Show Bar, Parker, seated in a wooden kitchen chair, did not even stand to solo. He looked both stunned and stoned. His playing was absolutely Bird, a succession of the very miracles I'd heard on records. The tone seemed even more pure, the slow numbers even more plaintive. Before I left I went up to shake his hand; haggard and pale, he never stood to take my hand, or even looked up.

•

One Friday afternoon I heard that Sonny Stitt was going to sit in with Gene Ammons that night at a dance hall on the east side. I was going to Wayne part-time and working full-time afternoons; I decided to skip work. All of my jazz buddies were busy with one thing or another, so I read in the library until it closed that Friday night and then walked the long blocks alone to find an enormous mob of kids my own age and younger waiting to get in, and it was worth the long wait. Stitt and Ammons battled good-spiritedly for hours, with Sonny mainly playing tenor with a huge tone and wonderful resourcefulness. A dance hall where no one danced. Forty years later, living in a tiny apartment in Nashville, I heard Sonny on the radio (a fortuitous event in Tennessee) and was inspired to try to catch the magic of that long-ago night:

> *Sonny was dazzling. The story went*
> *he'd just gotten out of Lexington*
> *the day before, was still clean, and could*
> *do it all on tenor and alto.*
> *When the last set ended I waited*
> *to thank him but so many people*
> *crowded around I gave up and left,*
> *walked the seven blocks to the streetcar,*
> *stood stamping in the cold, humming "My*
> *Funny Valentine" feeling happier*
> *than I ever expected to feel . . .*
> > *"It just gets you*
> *some kind of way," somebody once said.*
> *The man was talking about Ma Rainey,*
> *but it's all the same, music with words,*

music without words, words alone,
the city streets silently turning
toward the light, the still darkened houses
holding their tongues while a man dances
before them, content to be alone.

•

Dizzy's great band, the orchestra, playing on a Saturday night at the Paradise Theater, 1948 or '49. I walked in while they were playing "One Bass Hit": the brass went off like the Fourth of July, and then Dizzy himself came on, faster and higher than even Little Jazz. I'd never heard anything so powerful and disciplined.

In '51 in a huge place in Flint, size of a basketball stadium, I heard him again with John Lewis, Cecil Payne, and the wonderful tenor player James Moody, who insisted I was an FBI agent: he could tell by my shoes, the big, heavy, black clodhoppers I wore to work. I couldn't tell if Moody was serious or not; he and Cecil Payne accepted a ride back to Detroit in my little Ford two-door. By the time I got home the birds were singing. I was struck that night by the number and loveliness of the young groupies hanging around the band and the degree to which the musicians seemed to ignore them. Reminded me of Dylan Thomas at the 92nd Street Y in NYC, except Thomas did not ignore them.

•

An afternoon jazz concert on the second floor of the student union building at Wayne, a converted hotel used mainly to house students. Began with duets with Kenny Burrell and

Tommy Flanagan. Kenny, tall and shy, looked all of seventeen, and had already grown into that blues voice that would mark his playing. Tommy, short, compact, perhaps a few years older, barely looked at the audience. His mastery for so young a player was remarkable: one heard echoes of Art Tatum, Bud Powell, but he was less ornate than the former and more lyrical than the latter. He was then just twenty but already an accomplished artist.

In the second session they were joined by Pepper Adams, whom I'd known as a great wit and aspiring fiction writer (he'd said he hoped to be the F. Scott Fitzgerald of the bebop age, our age). When he opened up on the baritone, it was hard to believe that skinny, baby-faced boy wonder could get so much sound out of the great machine. Tall, bespectacled, with the complexion of a squid, Pepper looked like a candidate for a degree in mortuary science, but in fact he was already bringing to his playing the wit and drive that later marked his style.

Bess Bonnier and then Barry Harris replaced Tommy; Elvin Jones joined them on drums. What my classmates were in truth teaching me was that it was possible to be a kid from Detroit and an artist. And that if you worked hard enough at your art you could create original, beautiful works and just possibly live off your art. This was the first proof I saw it could be done, and those young musicians—several younger than I—were my early inspiration, living proof it could be done if you had the discipline and the desire; nothing was more obvious than that these young players knew their instruments and the history of the music they played, that they burned with the need to make music.

About that time Bess and I were classmates in a humanities course, and she and I wrote both music and poetry together. In fact it was the first time I showed my poems to more than one person. Her poems were better than my musical compositions; she taught me a lot about chord structures and musical accent and I helped her with the use of imagery. One time we were together on the Woodward streetcar when a woman, seeing Bess was blind, gasped and said, "Oh, my dear, you've lost your sight!" Bess: "How careless of me." Later Bess said, "She tried to make me feel like a penny waiting for change." I have never regretted not going to the University of Michigan or east to one of the Ivy League schools with their much-published English departments, for what I got from Wayne was unique and changed my vision of what was possible.

●

A summer evening in the early fifties, Bess and Elvin playing behind Stan Getz in an outdoor venue. Getz I'd already seen with the Woody Herman band at one of the big downtown picture palaces, and I'd fallen in love with his sound. Up close he looked like a movie star; up even closer you could tell he knew it. Bess was pissed off at him for playing the great man. The Getz sound was gorgeous, clearly cooler and slicker than any of the local tenor men, but the playing was minimal at best. He seemed determined to give just as much as he was being paid to give. Bess said he regarded her and Elvin with mild respect and the audience with contempt. The truth was, the audience was used to better stuff. It must have been hard on these brilliant young musicians, people like Bess, Elvin, Tommy, Kenny, Pepper, and Barry Harris, who knew they had the gift as well as the musicianship to play with people their own age and with big names but no more artistry. My classmates were in there for the long haul, and the best and the luckiest later made their

names, but what they seemed far more determined to do
was to make their music.

•

Kenny Burrell got a Sunday gig at some sort of hotel in
the downriver area of Detroit, a very unlikely place to hear
jazz; it was not as far downriver as Dearborn, where the
only blacks welcomed were those on their way to work at
the giant Ford Rouge plant. These were wonderful sessions,
for not only were all of the best of the local musicians pres-
ent, but the best of the visitors from the big bands would
drop in and were usually invited to play. And it was so inex-
pensive that even I could attend regularly. Curiously, the
Sunday I recall most clearly was one on which I arrived too
late to hear the music. Years later, living in Somerville, Mas-
sachusetts, and hearing of the death of Pepper Adams, I was
moved to record it in a poem.

THE WRONG TURN

There are those who will tell you
that the shortest way to get
to NYC is by way of Buffalo,
but back in 1949 if you left
Detroit at 2 a.m. when the clubs
were closing down, and the car—a '48
Studebaker that looked as though
it were going in two directions
at the same time—was owned by
Frenchman Jack, who along with
Pepper Adams was about to be

drafted, then why not misread
all the road signs and go by way
of Columbus, Ohio? Pepper was not
yet the greatest baritone saxophonist
—he was 21—but he was good,
so on a Saturday night he was working.
And he was tired. The Frenchman
had been out all day scrounging
money and supplies, so he was tired.

I, the driver, had been recovering
from a week of polishing plumbing parts,
which meant sleeping in until noon,
then clearing the debris out of my room,
which meant sweeping the rug with
precision and intensity so the reds
glowed like fire in the afternoon
and the Persian blues settled in.
Oh, how a man can love a rug
when it warms his only floor!
Thirty-five years ago, so I've forgotten
why I went to NYC and even
how I got back, I've forgotten
who I stayed with and whether
or not I walked the streets at night
wondering that so many lives
behind glass were not mine or if
I filtered through the bookstores
on Third searching for words that could
become mine so that I might say
what I did not yet have to say. I
recall that night I stood in the rain
for almost an hour, too shy even

*to speak to the girl who waited
beside me for the bus. I recall
that I arrived too late to hear
even a single number. The bar
was closed, so I watched Pepper
remove the mouthpiece and wipe
it carefully with a handkerchief
and stow the huge sax meticulously
in its garnet plush-lined case
which I carried out to the car
while he said goodbye to Kenny,
Elvin, and Tommy. In the dark
the Frenchman gave me a swig
of something hot and vile and I
almost gagged. They settled down
in the back, we decided to go
by way of Toledo, and they
talked and smoked and snoozed by turns
until there was silence. After
Toledo it was all two-lane,
no cars and no lights. The wet
fields of Ohio rushed by, rich
and autumnal, looming with presences
I couldn't imagine. I remember
the first sign that read "Columbus 45,"
and the next that said "Columbus 14,"
and I pulled over on the shoulder
of the road and turned on the map light.
Out of the back Pepper asked, "Where
are we?" and I answered, "Columbus"
because I thought that was where
we were. When Jack awakened
Pepper told him "Columbus."*

We all three began laughing,
until we cried we laughed so hard.

•

In 1953 I escaped a terrible marriage and a host of financial problems and so decided to pursue seriously a life in poetry; I wandered in the East for a time, and except for a night of Bud Powell on Fifty-Second Street saw almost no jazz and, lacking a record player, heard only what my car radio gave me. Out of money in the summer of '54, I returned to Detroit; and at Klein's Show Bar on Twelfth Street my first night home heard Milt Jackson. An extraordinary performance: good as he was on record, it was only a shadow of the playing I heard that night in a bar jammed to overflowing. During the months to come I heard many of the emerging jazz giants of our town: Paul Chambers, Frank Rosolino (who filled whatever room he played in without ever sounding too loud), and Elvin playing better than ever. I was working long days refinishing used bearings that were probably sold for new, so I had the time and money to discover Yusef Lateef and to hear Tatum out on Livernois. One night Kenny Burrell sat in and the place rocked with that Detroit blues sound destined to become more and more the signature of my city.

•

I've always envied the jazz musician, the ability to break into new song day after day, night after night, to be able to listen and answer to his or her fellow musicians. I love the fact that jazz has so much room for so many: you don't have to be Bird or Pres or Tatum to play with a genius;

the art leaves room for the good journeymen who do their best. By comparison poetry is so utterly solitary and interior. I think of young Wardell Gray playing at the Blue Bird with abandon and control, his artistry become body, muscles, breath, the stuff of life, maybe even digestion. I see in memory the whole person alive in the song, body and soul. Fantastic to experience something so total. The thrill of speaking through those ancient, inert metals mined from the earth and perhaps themselves stunned to be making music. What must it be like to make these *things*—this horn, this big-bellied wooden bass, this skin stretched over steel—make all that is lifeless come to life.

ABOVE JAZZ

A friend told me
He'd risen above jazz.
I leave him there.

> —*Michael Harper*

There is that music that the hammer
makes when it hits the nail squarely
and the wood opens with a sigh. There is
the music of the bones growing, of
teeth biting into bread, of the baker
making bread, slapping the dusted loaf
as though it were a breathing stone.
There has always been the music
of the stars, soundless and glittering
in the winter air, and the moon's
full song, loon-like and heard only
by someone far from home who glances

up to the southern sky for help and finds
the unfamiliar cross and for a moment
wonders if he or the heavens
have lost their way. Most perfect
is the music heard in sleep—the breath
suspends itself above the body, the soul
returns to the room having gone in dreams
to some far shore and entered water
only to rise and fall again and rise
a final time dressed in the rags of time
and made the long trip home to the body,
cast-off and senseless, because it is
the only instrument it has. Listen, stop
talking, stop breathing. That is music,
whatever you hear, even if it's
only the simple pulse, the tides
of blood tugging toward the heart
and back on the long voyage that must
always take them home. Even if you
hear nothing, the breathless earth
asleep, the oceans at last at rest,
the sun frozen before dawn and the peaks
of the eastern mountains upright, cold,
and silent. All that you do not hear
and never can is music, and in the dark
creation dances around the single center
that would be listening if it could.

A HISTORY OF MY
BEFUDDLEMENT

The teaching of poetry is a subject I should have a great deal to say about, since it was the means by which I mainly earned my living. I'd rather not calculate the number of classes I attempted to force-feed poetry long after I'd discovered that was folly. But what I have to give you is not the history of my own teaching but the ongoing history of what I have been taught, and that should delineate a history of my befuddlement. Be patient; the telling will not last nearly as long as the lessons. You will note, I don't think anyone taught me how to read poetry or even why I should feel it necessary to read poetry at all, though some assured me that without poetry not only my life but everyone's life would be less worthy. At times I believed this; worse still, I've said such things to undergrads who were trying to get their degrees in nursing, business administration, and hayseeding. (How did my students ever survive me?) If you live in poetry for sixty or more years, as I have, you can get an odd sense of its status. I have been foolish enough to ask people I've known outside the academy or the little cosmos of American poetry, people with whom I shared views on fiction, movies, music, politics, foreign cities, fountain pens, automobiles, wines, prizefighting, motorcycles, horse racing, "Who is your favorite poet?" This is one of the great showstoppers and conversation enders: often the question draws a clearing of the throat followed by a look of terror. At best one gets a blank stare, at worst an answer, which—hopefully—is a lie: Edgar Allan Poe.

•

I was first schooled in poetry when it was read to me by my mother who—although she was an immigrant from tsarist Russia with a tenth-grade education in the Detroit public schools—had a genuine love for what she regarded as poetry and especially enjoyed reciting it or reading it aloud to her ensnared six-year-olds. It was my father who sponsored her reading, she told us, a man she met and married when she was eighteen. He—also an immigrant from Russia—favored the Latin poets Juvenal and Persius, the satirists. (He died before I could discover how he'd found this poetry.) My mother's taste was at the other end of the spectrum: narrative and romantic and often schmaltzy. As I recall, the poem she read most often to us was "Jean Desprez" by Robert Service, which recounts how a barefoot French boy answers the pleas of a dying Zouave—crucified by the Germans—by giving him water. For his pains, the peasant boy is commanded to shoot the dying soldier or pay with his own life. Though "wild-eyed with fear," the boy, Jean Desprez, summons within a dozen lines the moxie to shoot his tormentor, a Prussian major, dead. By the time I was nine and had heard the poem many times I knew it was pure corn, and at that age I had less tolerance for corn than I do now; boys that age are realists immersed in the magical world of the ordinary. I'm not here to belittle my mother's taste; she was a single woman in her late twenties, intelligent, resourceful, faced with the task of raising three sons during the Great Depression. She drew strength and a sense of hope from writing most of us would laugh at, but that laughter would do nothing to diminish the authenticity of her experience. In 1941, when my twin brother and I were thirteen, she found

and purchased a copy of *A Stone, a Leaf, a Door,* a collec-
tion of fragments carved from the enormous body of the
fiction of her favorite novelist, Thomas Wolfe. These rhap-
sodic, and often pretentious, pieces—"O lost, and by the
wind grieved, ghost, come back again"—were in something
resembling modern American English, and my sense is I
found them more endurable, perhaps because they were
shorter and were fragments. After all, I was living in a series
of exalting and terrifying fragments while secretly trying to
capture the quality of my reverence and my terror in poems
of my own devising. How to describe what I was com-
posing? They were Whitmanian without Whitman, for I
had never read or even heard of Whitman—at Hampton
Elementary and Junior High School the poets I was taught
were Chaucer and Shakespeare and of course the seasonal
bard John Greenleaf Whittier, whose immortal poem
"Snow-Bound" my pushy sixth-grade classmate Gertrude
recited in toto to the applause of our teacher, Mrs. Tarbox.
By the time Gertrude got to the action   "Our buskins on
our feet we drew; / With mittened hands, and caps drawn
low, / To guard our necks and ears from snow, / We cut the
solid whiteness through"—half of us were comatose. Today,
I'm sure, things are much better: I would guess Robert
Hayden, another Detroiter, might be read—back then he
was there in the flesh, a graduate of my mother's grammar
school. These poems of mine, if poems they were, owed
their vocabulary to Wolfe and their form to the preachers I
heard on the radio, mainly southerners whose rhetoric was
positively biblical. I composed in and about the natural
world, which though I was a city boy struck me then as
miraculous and unknowable—in other words, exactly like
urban life, but less threatening and more distant and thus
more suitable material for my own voice. These so-called

poems were written without the models or the knowledge of true poetry, and thankfully they have vanished forever. Enter into my life Mrs. Paperno of Central High School, a lover of literature, a tiny, wise, and kindly woman, who one day read Wilfred Owen's "Arms and the Boy" to her English class, and when she was done reading it read it for a second time, and then said nothing. February of 1944. At the time I was more than a little anxious about my future. One of my classmates, wanting action, had lied about his age, enlisted in the marines, and was already dead on a Pacific atoll. My older brother was in England with the Eighth Air Force. Everything we read and heard on the radio or saw in the films conspired to tell us it was sweet and fitting to die for one's country. I've often wondered how Mrs. Paperno knew I neither wanted to kill or be killed in war or how she knew I had embarked on my first career as a poet. What could explain her offer to lend me the little collection of Owen to read over the weekend? I could lie and say those poems changed my attitude toward and my understanding of the importance of poetry. No, what it changed was my attitude toward myself. Poring over the poems of Owen, I discovered it was very possible that there was nothing contemptible about my response to the possibility I would become a combatant: fear was a natural response to war, and no matter what I might read or hear elsewhere, war was insane. Only later did I realize with what tact Mrs. Paperno had selected "Arms and the Boy," one of Owen's more obvious poems. I'm not sure a class of Detroit school kids with little familiarity with poetry would have been up to one of his great poems. There was a poem I missed back then which could have changed my notion of what my poetry might feel and sound like. Another ten years would pass before Stephen Spender, having glanced at a number

of my poems, ended his private discourse on Wilfred Owen
by suggesting I study "Inspection."

> *"You! What d'you mean by this?" I rapped.*
> *"You dare come on parade like this?"*
> *"Please, sir, it's—" "'Old yer mouth," the sergeant*
> *   snapped.*
> *"I take 'is name, sir?"—"Please, and then dismiss."*
>
> *Some days "confined to camp" he got,*
> *For being "dirty on parade."*
> *He told me, afterwards, the damned spot*
> *Was blood, his own. "Well, blood is dirt," I said.*
>
> *"Blood's dirt," he laughed, looking away,*
> *Far off to where his wound had bled*
> *And almost merged for ever into clay.*
> *"The world is washing out its stains," he said.*
> *"It doesn't like our cheeks so red:*
> *Young blood's its great objection.*
> *But when we're duly white-washed, being dead,*
> *The race will bear Field-Marshal God's inspection."*

A wonderful little drama, three characters speaking in their
proper voices in three acts. An enlisted man, an NCO, and
an officer as narrator. It's hard not to read the latter as Owen,
himself an infantry lieutenant. Owen, a modest, quiet man,
casts the officer as officious and naive. It's the enlisted man
who recalls his *Macbeth* and mentions the "damned spot,"
and must remind his lieutenant that they're not in a play in
which blood is dirt and a sign of guilt but in the real world,
where blood is life and vitality, and when you wash it away
you get absence, military order, true death. I don't know if

I was then ready for this poem, with its awareness of class and the languages of class.

•

Before I could graduate from high school the war ended, I was not drafted, and so I suddenly had to make a decision about what I might do with my life. I knew I did not want to go on doing factory work; I knew I didn't want to work in my Zayde's used-auto-parts business. I did what young people do who can't decide what to do with their lives: I enrolled in college. My first literature teacher assigned selections from the Oscar Williams anthology *A Little Treasury of Modern Poetry*. Inspired by T. S. Eliot, Stevens, Auden, I began my second career as an American poet.

•

There was a battle between the teaching methods of Dr. Gene Sax, the hottest professor in the English department, and Dr. A. D. Wooly, a battle that was perhaps fought only in my consciousness. Sax specialized in the most fashionable poets of that era, the seventeenth-century ironists, especially Donne, and the moderns. He used no notes but employed the blackboard ceaselessly as he paced back and forth before the class, stopping every few moments to add lines to his diagram of that day's poem; or if the poem was as dense as Stevens's "Sunday Morning," an entire hour could be consumed with the explication of a single passage. I watched as my classmates scribbled into their textbooks and the poem itself disappeared beneath a maze of notes and connecting lines. What was I being taught? Today I would have to say I learned how extraordinarily ingenious was Dr. Sax, the first navigator to bring the New Criticism to the old world of Detroit. Professor Wooly, who taught the romantics, thought nothing of assigning sixty pages of poetry for a single meeting. The class was expected to digest all of *Lyrical Ballads* between Monday and Wednesday and to pay special attention to the preface. None of the dozen students—Wooly, needless to say, was not a draw—seemed tempted to note his commentaries, which went something like "Here is the poet at the height of his powers" or "This goes to the heart of the matter." After reading aloud "Dejection: An Ode" he sat stunned by the power of the writing, or perhaps by his inability to articulate his response. Finally he told us Coleridge was incapable of writing a bad line, and then sat silently as the dozen of us filed out. Even I knew this was not superior teaching—I'd encountered that in Mrs. Paperno's classes—but somehow the unstated faith that if we were to welcome these poems into our hearts and minds they would achieve themselves without any insistence or pyrotechnics on his part won me over. I dropped Dr. Sax's class in favor of Wooly, who was content to let the poems teach themselves. What my classmates derived from this passivity I don't know; I know that when he remarked after a quiet reading of "Frost at Midnight" that "there is something here for each of us," I was certain I'd made the right choice. And I certainly had, for it was in Professor Wooly's class that I discovered the poetry and then the letters of John Keats; those letters became for me an essential source of knowledge about what it means to be a poet and what it means to be a person. Every few years I reread my favorites, and over sixty years they've never failed to surprise and enlighten. (If you get nothing else from this meandering piece, let it remind you to read or reread the letters of John Keats.)

·

In the fall of '53 Robert Lowell taught a graduate course in poetry writing and a seminar in modern poetry at the University of Iowa; in the spring semester John Berryman took his place and did likewise—thirteen aspiring poets had the good fortune to attend both of those classes, and I was one of them. People often ask me how Lowell taught, and now that his protector my friend Elizabeth Hardwick is dead, I can answer quite simply: badly. Lowell gave me the sense that there was a secret, a hidden key, to the reading of poetry. It was like a puritan's notion of salvation: you either deserved it or you didn't. On some days it seemed as though the secret had something in common with knowing what shoes to wear with a navy blue suit, what spirits to consume before dark, what wine to order with salmon, and whether the fish should be poached or baked. Yet we suffered him for fifteen weeks, during which we discovered he would never unlock the secret door to understanding. I can still hear him reading in his laconic and fraudulent southern accent this little poem by Housman, the last half-line of which he swallowed into silence:

> *Here dead we lie because we did not choose*
> *   To live and shame the land from which we sprung.*
> *Life, to be sure, is nothing much to lose,*
> *   But young men think it is, and we were young.*

"Someone tell me what the poet is getting at," Lowell said. This was near the start of the semester, so several of us raised our hands and offered an explication, each of which was answered with a barely perceptible turning of his head from side to side. This went on for at least ten minutes, during which Lowell read the poem a second time, even though each of us had the text before him. Finally in disgust our mentor turned to another poem by Housman, a poem featuring cherry blossoms, a poem I thought I understood, and once more the key was not forthcoming. By the time we got to John Crowe Ransom we'd learned there was no profit in attempting answers which only he possessed; but sadly Lowell had the patience to endure our silence. Perhaps his worst moment came on Ezra Pound night: again a slipshod reading, of sections of *Hugh Selwyn Mauberley,* accompanied by no explication. One student had the audacity to ask what were "the Burne-Jones cartons," which get a mention by Pound. A silence followed. Lowell stared wide-eyed above his reading glasses as though beholding something rare and miraculous. Finally, in amazement he said, "You don't know?" As the semester wore on, fewer and fewer of us showed up for class. I stayed to the bitter end, and felt exactly as Lowell wanted me to feel: honored to be in his company. To me he was and remains a superb poet. The poets I thought he would love—Hart Crane and Dylan Thomas—he urged us to avoid. In one sense he was urging us to avoid his own work, for none of us was in possession of so thrilling and exalted a voice or showed the talent to ever gain it. He prodded me to a rereading of Hardy—for which I am still thankful. "You can learn from him without being tempted to slavishly imitate him," he said, for he could surely hear the echoes of his own work in the poems I showed him. In the same vein he should have prodded me toward a study of William Carlos Williams; Lowell was still a young man, in his mid-thirties, and perhaps he hadn't discovered the wealth that was Williams. As the semester wore on, I discovered that one-on-one Lowell could be both helpful and encouraging; there was a real person inside the road show.

•

January saw the arrival of John Berrryman, who at the time was not a well-known poet. He had published only a single full-length collection, *The Dispossessed,* which had received modest attention. That winter there appeared a poem of his in *Partisan Review,* "Homage to Mistress Bradstreet" in its entirety, a poem that aroused extraordinary expectations, which Berryman would later fulfill. In his workshop John was ruthless and screamingly funny: everyone, which included three Pulitzer Prize winners-to-be, got leveled at one time or another. The seminar was even more memorable. How to describe it? Although John could be theatrical—in fact he had a difficult time *not* being theatrical—he never came close to saying, "This is the temple of poetry, and I am its high priest," to paraphrase Unamuno. His students knew it was true. For me there were two extraordinary high points. The first involved *Song of Myself.* John took three hours to go through the poem section by section and show us how the sections were linked thematically and imagistically to form "the single greatest poem ever written in the Western Hemisphere." The following week he presented the most powerful poetry reading I've ever heard, all of *Song of Myself.* Although he was a mental giant, John was not a powerful man physically or emotionally, and the reading left him near collapse. He got a standing ovation from the thirteen loyalists. The second high point involved his love for Dylan Thomas, the man and the poetry. This was near the very end of the semester, by which time all of us knew that John had been at St. Vincent's Hospital in Greenwich Village the night Thomas was hospitalized and died, and we knew too how haunted he was by his memory of that night. For the first time in class he began to talk about the poet himself, about the miracle of a self-educated boy from nowhere Wales, whose father was an underpaid schoolmaster, whose mother had no interest in books, how that man—who somehow miraculously remained a boy in the small, playful body of a man, who was in fact both man and boy at the same time—how that man became a great poet. "Yes," said John, "he was from the British Isles, but his story is completely American. Perhaps that is why Dylan's favorite living poet was Theodore Roethke, and perhaps that is why American poetry fell in love with Dylan." By this time John was close to tears. Quite suddenly he opened his book and announced, "I shall read one of the greatest, most audacious poems of this century, the finest poem in English to emerge from the nightmare of World War II, 'A Refusal to Mourn the Death, by Fire, of a Child in London.'" He began:

> *Never until the mankind making*
> *Bird beast and flower*
> *Fathering and all humbling darkness*
> *Tells with silence—*

And he stopped and looked up. "Justice, there is your paradox, your Donne and Ransom, he does them better than they do themselves . . ." And took up the reading again:

> *Tells with silence the last light breaking*
> *And the still hour*
> *Is come of the sea tumbling in harness*

And I must enter again the round
Zion of the water bead
And the synagogue of the ear of corn
Shall I let pray the shadow of a sound
Or sow my salt seed
In the least valley of sackcloth to mourn

The majesty and burning of the child's death. . . .

He stopped again. "Lafollette, there is the glorious syntax of your Milton, your Milton dragged bodily into our century in a poem worthy of the master . . ." By this time John was on his feet; I couldn't tell if it was sweat or tears that poured down his face . . .

I shall not murder
The mankind of her going with a grave truth
Nor blaspheme down the stations of the breath—

"My God, Petrie, is this religious—nay, *Christian* poetry of a caliber so rarely seen in our time? Your beloved Herbert is here in full force."

With any further
Elegy of innocence and youth.

Deep with the first dead lies London's daughter,
Robed in the long friends—

"Levine," he shouted, "here is the vision of your beloved Hardy in the sonority of a cathedral—only our Blake could do this, Dylan's great master. This single poem contains the history of English poetry—this is a miracle in which he gives the lie to the poem's title, for this is grief beyond grief." And he finished reading the poem:

> *Deep with the first dead lies London's daughter*
> *Robed in the long friends,*
> *The grains beyond age, the dark veins of her mother,*
> *Secret by the unmourning water*
> *Of the riding Thames.*
> *After the first death, there is no other.*

For the first time I truly understood that difficult poem, for John—even with all the stops and exclamations—had read it in such a way that the complex syntax was not only clear but totally justified, and the rhythmic power that drove the poem perfectly matched the exalted diction and the startling metaphors. Never again would I encounter so great a poem so perfectly presented. I've asked myself over the years: What made that hour so memorable (such perfect teaching of poetry, to tailor it for this occasion)? Let me sound foolish: It was John's love for the poem. And perhaps his regard for us, the thirteen somewhat talented, somewhat educated, and certainly devoted aspirants to poetry.

•

Let me for a moment step outside what has become a narrative. On that marvelous night John had said, "Levine, here is the vision of your beloved Hardy," and when I later thought about that I had no idea what he was talking about. Before John left Iowa City I asked him exactly what he'd meant. His answer was one word and for a time mystifying: "Transformations." Of course the poem was all about transformations, but where did Hardy come in? Mystifying only because I did not at the time know one of Hardy's greatest poems, "Transformations."

> *Portion of this yew*
> *Is a man my grandsire knew,*
> *Bosomed here at its foot;*
> *This branch may be his wife,*
> *A ruddy human life*
> *Now turned to a green shoot.*
>
> *These grasses must be made*
> *Of her who often prayed,*
> *Last century, for repose;*
> *And the fair girl long ago*
> *Whom I often tried to know*
> *May be entering this rose.*
>
> *So, they are not underground,*
> *But as nerves and veins abound*
> *In the growths of upper air,*
> *And they feel the sun and rain,*
> *And the energy again*
> *That made them what they were!*

And there it is, the vision of life growing out of death, of the inanimate giving birth to the animate, of life without end, as the fair girl whom the speaker tried to know now performs, by entering the rose, the act he was denied when she lived. This is such a quiet poem you can miss it; it was not Hardy's nature to thunder in his verse; in fact it quietly imitates a logical structure, the evidence is presented, and the conclusion is drawn: "So, they are not underground . . ." Perhaps because of its humility I am devoted to the Hardy, which operates on a smaller, private stage; Thomas purposely seeks a public stage and employs the imagery and rhetoric to justify it. It's a matter of taste; we have them both and needn't choose. The first poem I ever read by Dylan Thomas embodied the same biological mysticism. The first version of it was written for his twenty-second birthday, but he felt he didn't get it right for another two years:

TWENTY-FOUR YEARS

Twenty-four years remind the tears of my eyes.
(Bury the dead for fear that they walk to the grave in
    labour.)
In the groin of the natural doorway I crouched like a
    tailor
Sewing a shroud for a journey
By the light of the meat-eating sun.
Dressed to die, the sensual strut begun,
With my red veins full of money,
In the final direction of the elementary town
I advance for as long as forever is.

In Hardy's final volume, *Winter Words,* which was published shortly after his death in 1928, when he would have been eighty-nine, we find his final evocation of these sacred transformations.

PROUD SONGSTERS

The thrushes sing as the sun is going,
And the finches whistle in ones and pairs,
And as it gets dark loud nightingales
　　In bushes
Pipe, as they can when April wears,
　　As if all Time were theirs.

These are brand new birds of twelvemonths' growing
Which a year ago, or less than twain,
No finches were, nor nightingales,
　　Nor thrushes,
But only particles of grain,
　　And earth, and air, and rain.

One poet in his youth, another in his final days, both with such similar visions, both triumphant, both in command of their craft, and in their individual voices sounding not the least like each other.

•

Back to the prosaic and to Levine. It was 1954; ahead lay marriage and children, those hostages to fortune likely to derail a poet, and, even more dangerous, a year as a student of Yvor Winters at Stanford. Winters was famous for crushing would-be poets. For those of you too young to have had the opportunity to study with him, my advice is read and reread *In Defense of Reason* and the essays that preceded it, for you will encounter a brilliant, original, and perceptive reader of poetry. In 1957 as a classroom teacher Winters was

94

hopeless; he often read us his own essays from the textbook, read them in a voice that could put mermaids to sleep. Mr. Winters—as I knew him—and I were very comfortable together. He knew from my poetry—he had chosen me for a fellowship on the basis of submitted poems—who I was and what my aims were; he knew perfectly well I didn't want to become a Wintersean poet. The day after I fell asleep in his seminar in English poetry he told me I was no longer obliged to attend. His love for poetry was the equal of Berryman's, except with Winters there was a lot less to love, as he had dismissed so much good and great poetry from his private canon, and each year more poems failed to make the cut. With justification, Winters felt the Eastern establishment belittled his work. When he received a telegram informing him he'd been honored with the Bollingen Prize his response was "too little, too late." Unlike Berryman, Winters was not comfortable with an audience. For one thing, he was a very awkward man, physically and socially; he didn't care for Stanford undergraduates, felt they were too rich and too inexperienced. And he suffered from grade-A paranoia; at times he even felt students had been sent by Tate & Ransom to torture him. One-on-one he could be amazing. He had only two students in his poetry-writing class, both of us on fellowships. To say the least he was unkind to my classmate, a young Methodist minister and a perfect target for the attacks of a confirmed agnostic.

•

Winters loaned me a copy of *Les Amours jaunes* by Tristan Corbière as well as a French dictionary, but my years of high-school French failed me, as Winters knew they would.

So one afternoon he took me through his favorite, the long ballad of St. Anne of the Pardons, reading it first in French, not in his usual classroom drone but with a lightness and delicacy I hadn't imagined him capable of. Then he went through it in English, translating from scratch and filling in the background necessary to a comprehension of the central occasion of the poem, a local Breton holiday celebrating the mother of the Virgin Mary, who according to local legend was a Breton. Then a second and equally delicate reading in French. This was an extraordinary gift from an aging poet to a beginning poet. He was a truly serious and generous man, one who found so few occasions during which he could act out his generosity. And this was great teaching: a poem was given to me in a language I barely grasped—Breton French—and inspired me and stayed with me for decades. I find it difficult to describe the power and the beauty of the moment when the poem opened in something approximating its fullness. I received a similar gift eight years later in a village south of Barcelona. At the time I was just learning Spanish, when the poet and translator Hardie St. Martin took me slowly and patiently through "Nanas de la Cebolla" (Lullabies of the Onion) by Miguel Hernández, the greatest single poem to rise from the horror of the Spanish Civil War.

•

In the spring of 1959 at Fresno State I finally got a chance to teach twentieth-century poetry. In this initial class in poetry, I felt responsible for a presentation of the majors: Frost, Yeats, Stevens, Eliot, Williams, Moore, and D. H. Lawrence. One afternoon in late March I was in the middle of an explication of Eliot's "Gerontion"; as I paced back and forth in front of the class I found myself distracted by four plum trees in full bloom in the courtyard below the business building. (That was where the administration felt the teaching of literature could do the least harm.) "Will you look at that!" I said. When I turned to the class I realized no one had heard me, which meant that no one had been listening. For how long I had no idea. I shouted at the class, "Hey, wake up and look at this!" The students, all twenty-some, rose from their seats and came to the window. "Those are plum trees," one student said, with all the enthusiasm of a reptile. We are in the world of Chinese poetry, I thought. Once we returned to "Gerontion" I couldn't go on. My first vision of plum trees had seized the day. Someone with a greater sympathy for Eliot's Anglo-Catholic poetry might easily have held their attention, might have inspired the kids. (Perhaps you're thinking Fresno State, you're thinking ag students, you're thinking second-rate at best. Since '58 I've taught all over—Tufts, Brown, Iowa, Princeton, Columbia, NYU, Vanderbilt, Houston, U of North Carolina, the National University of Australia, even at UC Berkeley, and my best students were at humble Fresno State.) No, it was I who failed Eliot and the students. My students had picked up on my own lack of enthusiasm for the text. Thus I learned early never to teach anything I felt lukewarm about. This has caused me some trouble: at Tufts a bright student, the guitar-wielding son of a colleague, demanded to know why we were reading Edward Thomas and D. H. Lawrence instead of Ezra Pound. I explained that there were several anti-Semites on the faculty who I was sure would be delighted to teach Pound. He said, "So we have to read this shit!" I recalled Frost's encomium on teaching: your first obligation is to yourself, your second to the material you teach, your third to the students. What I said in response I'll not repeat. It was terrible.

•

In 1976, while traveling in England with a group of American poets, I was asked to give a short reading at a workmen's club in Nottingham. The evening was incredibly hot—not just hot for England, really hot—and the windows were open to admit the usual street noises. I had no mike, and to my surprise the place was jammed with perhaps sixty or seventy men who appeared to listen attentively. When I finished, they applauded. The hostess from the British Arts Council thanked me and asked for questions, something that often invites disaster. A large fellow, in gray, heavy wool trousers and suspenders over a T-shirt that did nothing to hide his capacious belly, rose and said in a Midlands accent, "What you read was very interesting, Mr. Levine, and I mean no disrespect, but it's not poetry. I know poetry and that's not it." No one except the hostess seemed startled by what might have passed for rudeness; as an experienced reader in Fresno and Berkeley, I was used to much worse. He went on: "Might I recite a true poem?" I told him to go ahead, and we heard a stirring presentation of Kipling's "Danny Deever." Was he wrong? Was this true poetry? Who am I to say?

•

Let me close with a lesson I received for free from one of your finest poets. Some years ago I was in southern Arizona in the town of Bisbee as a performer at a poetry conference.

The only attraction I found besides the poets was the largest hole in the ground I'd ever seen. It had been left by the mining corporation that robbed the place of several of its resources. Along with two other poets I was assigned a panel on "The Value of Poetry in the Contemporary World." The youngest of the three went first and at great length made it clear she thought that without a frequent immersion in the sacred texts of poetry one would lack a motive for being, a sense of beauty, a moral compass. I drifted into silence. Robert Duncan did not. He took issue, not with the tone but with the content. He made it perfectly clear he knew many, many people who never bathed in the ocean of poetry and possessed a sense of beauty, a reason to be, and a moral compass. "Some people," he said, "do not twig to poetry, they may be inspired by things others don't care for—the operas of Wagner, the novels of Proust, the ballets of Merce Cunningham, the stories of Katherine Mansfield, the philosophical writing of Schopenhauer, the paintings of Francis Bacon. Perhaps they love the beauty of design, of Tiffany vases or of machinery, V-8 engines or drop forges. I think we would do poetry a favor if we stopped trying to shove it down the throats of those for whom it has no connection or resonance." And then he added, "But don't forget, if absolutely nothing turns you on, stirs you body and soul, you are in trouble." I took him seriously.

Have I bored you? I hope not. Have I befuddled you? I certainly hope so.

A DAY IN MAY

Los Angeles, 1960

A few days ago I got a call from a reporter from the *San Francisco Chronicle* informing me that my old friend Thom Gunn had died in his sleep, probably of a heart attack. This fellow had the task of writing his obituary, and somehow he'd gotten my name. I was stunned into silence for a time. I couldn't believe it: the Thom I saw in my mind's eye was so young, energetic, and surrounded by an aura of mystery I'd never penetrated, and also so generous and loving. The guy in the motorcycle jacket and jeans I'd met in '57 at Stanford, tall and slender, a few years younger than I but so much more a man of the world and moving with the very grace of his marvelous poems, those poems I knew before I knew him and had made me want to know him. I began to answer the reporter's questions: how had I met him, what had he meant to me, to American poetry. The more I talked about him, the more I wanted to talk about him, for he had been such a fixed star in my poetry world, someone I learned from, not only how to write poems about the world I had lived in but also how to face rejection. After thirty minutes the reporter seemed to awaken and said he had to go off to write this article, time was getting short, and then he was gone, and I was alone with my remembrances. My mind drifted to that day I first got to know him well, the first day I truly shared with him, a day I hadn't mentioned to the reporter. For me it was an unusually long and rich day in Los Angeles that involved three other writers. Now all of them are dead, and I'm the only one left to tell the story. Or perhaps I should say tell the story of my version of that day, tailored and trimmed by imagination and memory.

For me the day began at five a.m., for I had to drive from Fresno to Los Angeles to collect Thom and John Berryman at the LA airport. They were flying down from Berkeley, where Thom was a regular at the university and John was teaching for the spring quarter. The three of us were scheduled to read at Los Angeles State College (as it was then called) that day in the early afternoon. At the time I'd given only a few public readings, and I found the prospect of this day both daunting and exciting. Their plane was scheduled to arrive at 10:15, and much to my surprise I made it on time, driving a terrible Chevy I'd requisitioned from Fresno State, where I was completing my second year of teaching. (I had serious doubts my old Ford would have made it at all.) I hadn't seen Berryman since I'd said goodbye to him at the Iowa City airport in the spring of '54, and much had transpired since. For one thing we'd both married for the second time, but now I had three sons. John too had married for a second time, this venture to a woman named Levine with whom he'd fathered his only son. He had also published his breakthrough volume, *Homage to Mistress Bradstreet,* which had received some of the acclaim it deserved.

In other ways nothing had changed. John was still clean-shaven, dressed in semi–Brooks Brothers style which failed to hide his gangly build and terrible posture. Thom, incredibly handsome, dark-haired, hawk-nosed in a forties-British-film-star manner, was doing his best to look American, sporting a baseball cap and wearing a red jacket the lettering of which spelled "Forty-Niners" in the appropriate script. When the two poets emerged from the plane and saw me waiting, Thom—flashing a huge smile—yelled,

"See, what did I tell you!" John looked stunned. "Levine," he shouted at me, "what have you done to yourself? You've shrunk!" It seems that on the plane the two poets had argued over my relative size, John insisting I was enormous, the size of a Chicago Bears linebacker, and Thom just as certain I was a relatively small man, shorter than either of them—which I was—and no heavier than Thom. (At the time I was 5'10" and around 165 pounds or less, pretty much what I am now, only the pounds are in different places. Why John remembered me as this brute is another story I'd just as soon not tell.) In the years I'd known John he'd never taken being wrong very well, and this occasion was no exception. He needed something quick to recover from the shock of my shrinkage, which he feared was related to some life-threatening medical problem. "Does this godforsaken airport have a bar or have we burrowed further into incivility than even Berkeley?"

Fortunately I knew the location of a stunning bar in the airport near where I was parked, a towerlike structure the top of which turned slowly to reveal clouds of collecting pollution through which the airplanes rising and descending broke each few minutes. Thom—never much of a drinker—ordered a glass of orange juice, I went for seltzer on the rocks, and unfazed John asked for a double martini and then began to explain his new theory of drink. "When last I saw you, Levine, my drinking was not in hand, for which I'm sorry, but since then I've mastered the art." And he went on to explain the cardinal points of this new approach. "To begin with, you never, *never* drink in bars; it's a huge waste of money, and one is liable to meet all sorts of unsavory characters while inebriated and possibly defenseless." Ordering a second martini, he seemed perfectly apt at ignoring where he was. "I went to the master drinker, William Empson," he said, "and he explained that it was quite simple: one discovered what was ideal for one and drank that and only that. Quite simple. In the morning one fills a carafe with one's chosen spirits, and when the day wears on and it's empty one's drinking for that day is over. OVER completely!" he shouted in that strange high voice of his that dogs could barely hear. How large a carafe in his case? I inquired. "In my case one litre," he said. In his crazy accent you could hear the English spelling.

Our host for the reading was the poet Henri Coulette, and so we drove to his apartment in South Pasadena. Henri had met John when I did, when we studied with him in a wonderful poetry-writing class he taught at the University of Iowa back in '54, the only class of its kind he ever taught and certainly one of the finest anyone ever taught. John had a yen to see Forest Lawn cemetery, and Henri—a native Angelean and the only one of us who'd ever visited it—directed us to the place. Upon entering the grounds we found a man busily whitewashing an enormous reproduction of Michelangelo's *David*. "The perfect piece of art for a cemetery," remarked John. "Being dead isn't bad enough, they have to remind you of what life looked like at its most glorious." The place was enormous and confusing, so Henri went off to find some sort of map or guide and returned with a young man dressed in funereal black who pretended to be familiar with the name of John Berryman, the eminent American poet. "You may visit any part of the park, merely remember to be respectful of the graves. Picnicking is not allowed." John wanted to know where the most famous of the old-time film stars were buried. "Up there," the young man said, pointing to a hilltop, "where the views are most spectacular." "Do you expect the deceased to enjoy the view?" John said. No, that luxury was

there for the mourners. It turned out there was a poets' cor-
ner in the cemetery, to which we immediately headed, but
among the gravestones was not a single name any of us had
ever encountered before. John was disgusted and wanted
out immediately. He wanted to know where they'd found
these women of both sexes with three names and how they
had dubbed them poets. Thom patiently talked him out of
returning to the young man and challenging him to pres-
ent us with their credentials as poets. "John, the guy is just
doing his job." "When your countrymen have a poets' cor-
ner, as they do in Westminster Abbey, they put Milton and
Dryden in it. Can't we do better than these nonentities who
never published in anything but local newspapers? I'm for-
getting vanity presses. One mustn't forget vanity presses."
Thom then recalled asking to see the tomb of Andrew
Marvell—an early hero—in the great cathedral of York. "It
took me almost an hour to find anyone who'd heard the
name." It turned out this old cleric for whom the name had
resonance told him with disgust how Marvell's remains had
long ago been stolen for Westminster Abbey.

Henri, who had raised the money for today's events as
well as organized the program, explained how it would
work. Thom and I would share the first forty minutes, and
then Berryman would read for forty minutes. Christopher
Isherwood, who was teaching a course at LA State entitled
"Auden and Others" ("Mainly a few hours of fascinating
chat," said Henri), had asked to introduce Thom, who
appeared very touched by this information. He said he'd
met Isherwood, presented him with his most recent book,
but had no idea he'd read it. Henri would do the honors
for John and me. Being the less experienced reader and cer-
tainly the least well known of the group, for I hadn't pub-
lished a book yet, I asked to go first. The event would take

place in the college theater to an audience that Coulette estimated at five hundred or more. Isherwood had asked to be allowed to take us all to lunch at some swanky place in Hollywood once the reading was over.

While I paced nervously backstage, a little tanned and muscular man in short sleeves—no doubt a stagehand, I thought—with the most gorgeous smile in the world wished me luck in what I took to be an Italian accent. I was too distracted to hear any of Coulette's introduction. The lighting was dramatic: the audience in darkness, a single spot on the reader, who stood behind a podium. The sound system was superb, and within a single poem I warmed to the task and didn't do badly. (My previous reading with Gary Snyder in North Beach had been a disaster. For me—not for Gary, who read splendidly.) I then found Thom's seat in the front row to watch the Italian stagehand introduce Gunn. He had donned a blue, double-breasted blazer and was none other than Christopher Isherwood.

Thom had then and for the rest of his career a very modest style of reading; he read with enough emotion to demonstrate his seriousness, but he never went over the top. He spoke little between poems, enough to mark a pause between one poem and another; he clarified whatever references required clarification, but unlike many readers today he never spoke so much that the poem itself came as an anticlimax, since you'd already learned what was coming. That day I was still too far into my own reading to catch the first few poems, and besides I knew the poems so well I could have recited them, for most of what he read was from a book that had deeply influenced me, *The Sense of Movement,* his second book. When he came to the poem "My Sad Captains" and several other poems from a volume-to-be, I came suddenly awake, for these were some of the most stunning syllabic poems ever written, and they marked a new departure in his work. Thom had already found a style that perfectly suited his nature, and he never let his private life intrude on his readings. He fulfilled my notion of what a poet's stage presence should be. Years later I heard him laugh over a long-remembered reading by Marianne Moore; he claimed he didn't know when she was explaining the poem, examining her life, gossiping, or simply reading what was on the page. After a while he thought her explanations—which often came in the middle of the poem—were merely the portions of the poem she'd neglected to write. That day Thom was very much at ease, very much the same man onstage as the one offstage, and he put the audience at ease.

An audience at ease was exactly what Berryman did not want. It's hard to say what he wanted besides their full attention. After Coulette's lavish introduction, John came out slowly, stared at the audience, and murmured "My heavings" into the mike. He seemed genuinely moved to be standing before such a large and totally silent audience, and he began with an anecdote. "The last reading I gave was in a basement classroom on the campus at UC Berkeley, no doubt arranged by either the Dean of Death or my first wife. There was not a shred of publicity, though all the readers—Thom, Louis Simpson, and I—are all currently on the faculty. As I told the audience of twelve—which included the readers—I had no idea why I was so nervous, since there were more students in my nine a.m. class when the girls showed up." Pause. "But then the girls never showed up." All this delivered in that strange breathless voice that hovered between a tenor and an alto in his Ivy League fraudulent-English accent. At any moment he seemed on the verge of collapse from the burden of so much emotion. The audience roared, and without further comment he launched into the recitation of a Chinese poem in Chinese, which he did not bother to translate. Then to Jon Silkin's little-known, extraordinary poem "Death of a Son (who died in a mental hospital aged one)" and from there to one of Blake's less-well-known songs, "Night." As Coulette later remarked, John had a way of reading that made you think you were encountering the poem for the first time. The audience was utterly silent, hypnotized or awed. Then he presented a group of poems from his recently published pamphlet "'His Thoughts Made Pockets' & 'The Plane Buckt.'" These were the first composed poems of what would later be called *The Dream Songs,* and we—the poets in the audience, perhaps the entire audience—were stunned by the originality, the combination of wit and seriousness, and the sheer vitality and resourcefulness of the writing. Before he read them he gave us a short explanation: "I want this to be clear. What you are about to hear is not autobiography. This fellow Henry, who occupies center stage in many of these poems, is not to be confused with me or Mr. Coulette or any other Henry you happen to know. He is a poetic invention, not of the stature of Hamlet or Lear, but unlike those inventions he is both contemporary and entirely mine." Then John threw himself into the poems totally. It was obvious he believed they were what he was meant to write, what he had been preparing for all his poetic life. When he finished, to tumultuous applause, he seemed completely spent. Before the lights came on, Isherwood, who was seated behind me, tapped me on the shoulder and informed me that my mother was in the audience—"Charming woman," he said. He seemed to think this was amazing, as if she'd come all the way from Detroit to hear me and not from Culver City, five miles away. Or perhaps he thought it was ordinary; he had a way of saying things that made them sound very special.

And then the lights did come on, and as I made my way out of the theater I was assailed by an enormous black man who had in tow a gorgeous, tall woman of uncertain ethnicity; she could easily have been a Samoan princess out of a Jon Hall movie. Once she opened her mouth it was clear she was an American and, I would guess, a drama major. The man and woman had made a wager on which of the other two readers was English. The man, who was actually the poet Michael Harper, then a student of Coulette's, insisted it was Gunn who was English. The woman was just as sure it was Berryman. I wanted to side with her, but it was my sad duty to inform her that Gunn was the only true Englishman. She was stymied. Where had John gotten that accent? "He was born in Oklahoma," I said, which, though true, explained nothing. At the time I was as puzzled as she.

We were then taken outside in a group, the five of us, and photographed for the college publicity department against the backdrop of one of the more hideous state buildings. (The various branches of the California State University system look designed by some architect who apprenticed under Mussolini's cultural minister and failed. I have since tried without success to obtain a copy of one of the photographs, but they seem to have vanished.) From there we were whisked to a tony Hollywood restaurant of Isherwood's choosing. Berryman immediately ordered another martini while ogling the voluptuous woman who had seated us. She seemed to have a particular affection for Isherwood, addressing him as Christopher. The contrast between Christopher and John was severe. John was all motion: tall, badly coordinated, he seemed to be moving in several directions at the same time, always with a cigarette in one hand and demanding attention. I would not say he was singularly ugly. He was funny looking; there was too much unaccounted-for space between his upper lip and his nose, and since he rarely stopped talking, one's eyes were drawn to that spot. Isherwood, by contrast, was short, compactly built, and incredibly handsome, the sort of looks one associates with an Olympic oarsman; and though he was lined around the eyes, which were wide and beautiful, he was one of those men who look young until they are suddenly truly old. (The British film actor Tom Courtenay is an example.) He was also deeply tanned from his morning ocean swims; he had the aura of true health, both inner and outer. In a word, he was beautiful. Furthermore, unlike Berryman, he seemed to have no particular need to talk.

Once he got his martini, and then a second one, John seemed to have no particular interest in eating. Thom and I ripped into a seafood platter that was the specialty of the house. Christopher was sorry that nothing of interest was going on at the studio or he would have gladly taken us on a tour. He then told a story of the last time he'd taken a poet on a tour of the studio, the poet being a young Robert Lowell. They happened upon a set of a Jayne Mansfield movie in which she was receiving a back massage, clad only in a towel that covered her from the waist down. For some reason the filming was interrupted, and Miss Mansfield sat up, revealing her breasts, which Isherwood then described as large and, he said, holding both hands out high above his chest, "I suppose the way men like them." Within less than a minute a wardrobe mistress covered her with a bathrobe. Christopher then took Lowell on the set of several other films and then to lunch at the studio dining room, which was packed with film stars. Lowell seemed curiously distracted and finally asked, "You don't suppose we could return to the Mansfield set?" Isherwood assured him that in all his years in Hollywood he'd never seen anything quite like what they'd observed that morning. Lowell still insisted. When they returned to the set, they were in the process of filming another scene in which Ms. Mansfield was fully clothed. Lowell called it quits.

Berryman was curiously silent during the telling of this tale, and I thought he was simply worn out from the reading, which had been incredibly intense. Soon the stunning hostess who had first directed us to our table appeared at Christopher's side to inform him that a car was waiting for him from the studio. He was being summoned back to work. "I should be grateful, they gave me half of the day off, but I feel I would like to stay with all of you," he said. "Please stay as long as you like, and eat and drink whatever you like. It's all on me— or rather the studio." He assured us that we were in the capable hands of the stunning hostess, who would see to all our needs within reason. And he was gone.

No sooner had he left than Berryman announced, "It's not fair." Thom asked him what wasn't fair. "Did you see how that gorgeous woman couldn't take her hands off him, and he couldn't give a fig for any woman. Here I am, totally enthralled with her, and she doesn't know I'm alive. He has it all, and I have nothing." Thom tried to talk him out of it. "John," he said, "Christopher is a name in Hollywood. He comes here frequently, he comes here with celebrities from the studio. Of course they pay special attention to him. It means nothing about you—it means he's Christopher Isherwood." But Berryman clung to his funk, insisting life wasn't fair, especially to him. Finally Coulette suggested we visit a particular bar in downtown LA that would be full of attractive women who would fall all over John, so off we went in Coulette's Jaguar sedan. Unfortunately, when we arrived at the bar it was almost empty; but somehow Berryman's mood had shifted upward noticeably when a tall blond woman came to our booth to take our orders. "You could make me very happy," said John. "Do you know how?" The woman had the good sense to say nothing. "All you have to do is tell me that that man"—he pointed at the bartender, who seemed half asleep beneath the silent television screen—"tell me he knows how to fix a proper double martini." That she could do, she assured him, and the rest of us breathed a sigh of relief.

It must have been in the hilarity that followed John's first taste of his martini, which he claimed was, though not perfect, by far the best he'd encountered west of the Hudson, and he had encountered numberless examples—it must have been in that moment that I agreed to do something remarkably stupid, something I should never have done. Thom had told Berryman that I could do an imitation of him that was almost perfect. Berryman said, "I've heard you've been passing yourself off as me, Levine. It won't do; any fool can tell a Berryman from a Levine. For one thing, since you've shrunk you're too short to be a Berryman, though I must admit you've done a credible job of foisting off your terrible poems on the even more terrible editors of literary magazines." When dealing with individual poems of mine, John could say remarkably useful and insightful things—he was an absolutely superb practical critic, the best I had then encountered—but he took pleasure in referring to my work as a whole as my "terrible poems." Perhaps, hearing that remark for the twentieth time, I was more than a little peeved; in any case I launched my voice into that particularly hysterical style that marked his reading and gave him back one of his favorite passages from

"Song of Myself." Thom exploded with laughter: "Perfect, Phil—you've got him perfectly!"

Berryman simply rose from the booth and left the bar, though where he might go in downtown Los Angeles, a city he did not know, was anyone's guess. "That was a mistake," Coulette said, and I knew he was right. Thom wondered if we ought to go looking for him, sure that he could be lost in five minutes. Coulette was more sanguine. "Stay right here," he said, "he'll be back in no time." And of course he was right. In less than ten minutes John was back; he'd purchased a box of Band-Aids at a drugstore and was determined to plaster one across my mouth, something I was not about to let him do. I apologized for what I'd done and claimed it was not meant as an imitation but rather as a cruel parody, which only demonstrated the weakness of my character. "You did not sound like me, not for a second! Your mouth should be sewn shut forever for taking your master in vain!" I assured him I'd learned my lesson and henceforth I would never take his name or his voice in vain.

By this time we'd tired of the empty bar, and the other three of us were more than a little exhausted by John. It was now mid-afternoon, and John wondered if it was possible to visit one of the storied hangouts of the beats, who were known to "infest the city." He was immensely curious about these characters, who'd seized so much attention and had managed to pass themselves off as artists and poets, although as far as he could tell none of them could write anything worth reading. "They don't understand Whitman, they imitate his worst mannerisms; they don't understand Buddhism, but they have mastered the art of self-promotion." He was reminded of a remark F. R. Leavis had made regarding the Sitwells, which he quoted: "The Sitwells belong to the history of publicity rather than of poetry." Ginsberg he especially belittled, and I wondered if he wasn't a little jealous of someone who was quickly becoming the spokesperson for an entire generation. Coulette knew exactly the place where John could view the beats in their native habitat. It was in Venice, close to the sea. As we headed west, Thom asked to be dropped off. I wasn't sure if it was because he was worn out by John's shenanigans or simply had better things to do. I also knew that Thom had great regard for some of the so-called beat writers, whom he knew personally in San Francisco, especially Robert Duncan. In any event we dropped him off in Santa Monica and headed south to Venice.

The place we arrived at was a huge barnlike structure only a few hundred yards from the Pacific. It looked as though it had been furnished from a Salvation Army warehouse. Beer, wine, and soft drinks were all they served, although the place reeked of pot. Fortunately they carried Ballantine ale, one of John's favorites, and we went off to inspect the premises. What we first stumbled into was a huge, sparsely furnished post-Victorian living room with several large chairs from which the stuffing was leaking and two old couches that faced each other at a distance of six feet or so. On one sat a young man, clean-shaven, quite presentable, and on the other, facing him, a woman of about his age wearing Levi's and a white blouse. Neither was reading, although between them was a low table stacked with books. In fact they didn't seem to be doing anything at all, and it seemed unlikely that they'd been speaking to each other or ever intended to do so. "Have you two been introduced?" John said. "If not, I would be more than glad to do the honors." The woman, who was extremely attractive even without a touch of makeup, said nothing; she neither looked away nor looked at any of us, but merely continued to stare off at nothing we could see. The young man finally said, "Thanks, but don't bother."

The place was quite warm. John removed his jacket, rolled up his sleeves over his slender forearms, and, pacing back and forth between the two young people, began to lecture the air. "This is what is meant by being 'beat.' One is reduced to complete passivity, to accepting as little as possible. While this man in any other circumstances would make some sort of overture to this very handsome woman, or this woman might acknowledge his presence or ours or even flirt a teeny bit—even though that is a practice banished to the previous century—these two do nothing at all. And they do it with great determination and, I suppose, skill. They are about the work of being 'beat,' and the poetry written by them or about them or for them will do exactly as much as they are presently doing, which is to say nothing." At last the young man looked up at John and said, "Yup, you got it."

Berryman soon ran out of patience with them. He was also sure the beer had been watered or, worse, was not what it was advertised to be. "Beer is at best not much," he said, "but I think this was brewed in Munich in 1944, and the Bavarians used sawdust instead of grain." He wanted whiskey; it seemed to him years since he'd had a real glass of whiskey. Coulette said he had an unopened bottle of Chivas at his place, and John thought that might just hold him until dinner. At the time Henri was living in a second-floor apartment in South Pasadena with his wife, Jackie, a public-school teacher. Just as we were about to turn down his street, the police pulled over the car ahead of us, a convertible carrying two suntanned young surfer types in the front seats. We stopped behind the two cars. Shirtless, the blond driver leaped out of the car to face one of the cops, who immediately pushed a revolver into his bare belly and forced him to bend over the hood of his car. John, who was sitting next to Coulette in the front seat, shouted, "Stop it! He's going to kill that man for driving without his shirt on!" He seemed perfectly serious and enraged. "These are storm troopers! They should wear black shirts like the SS!" He'd never seen anything like it in America, but he'd heard all about the incredible brutality of LA cops, and now he could see that what he'd heard was true. Coulette assured him that he'd lived in Los Angeles most of his life and had never seen anything like this. "It's exactly like what Isherwood told us about taking Lowell through the studio," Henri said. "Once in his life he sees a naked woman on the set, but Lowell thinks it's a daily occurrence. The visitor comes to Los Angeles, and the city does its worst to be LA . . ." Berryman was unconvinced. "Levine, you saw it. You're from Detroit, a place notorious for brutality. Did you ever see anything like this?" No, I hadn't, but then men didn't go around half-naked in Detroit. I'd seen police brutality; it just looked different, and it wasn't out in this dazzling sunshine. I told him I'd seen a cop beating a man while another cop held a gun on him, but that was in jail. It wasn't out there for the whole world to see. Berryman was shaken and claimed he needed a drink badly; the Chivas would do, although he'd switched to bourbon as a regular drink.

How did the day end? I too began drinking, and since I lacked the capacity of either John or Henri, events from here on get hazy. I know the three of us and Henri's wife, Jackie, went out to a steakhouse for dinner. Feeling sick from a sudden attack of tachycardia, I went out into the alley behind the restaurant and threw up. Later Henri came out to check on me, and I told him the worst was over, which was true: my heartbeat had returned to normal. (Tachycardia is something I've lived with since I was a child.) Someone picked up the check, probably Henri. We stopped off at Coulette's apartment, which was near to John's hotel. Jackie Coulette, who operated as Henri's publicist, wanted Henri to show John a poem he'd recently published in *The Paris Review,* a superb poem about a loner who lives in a huge park in LA. Curiously, Berryman misread the poem; he seemed to think it was written in syllabics. Henri and I had both been experimenting with syllabics for some years, but this poem was not one of those experiments. We then endured a drunken lecture on the proper use of syllabics, though Coulette's poem was clearly in rhymed tetrameter, and as far as I could tell, John—who'd never written syllabics—knew nothing about the form. Jackie excused herself, sensibly, and went off to bed. An hour later we wound up at the hotel where John was staying, the Green Hotel in Pasadena—no longer extant. When we arrived, the revelers from a high-school graduation dance were leaving. Most of the men looked as drunk as John, while the women were stunning in their satiny gowns that revealed their tanned shoulders and a good measure of their young bosoms. John simply stood and stared until the last of them had left. Once again he cursed his rotten luck for being so ugly and so old. (It was impossible to know if he was serious. At the time, though badly used, he didn't look any older than he was, forty-six, and in possession of his hair and still quite slender and wiry. He had once congratulated himself for not being handsome and assured me that beautiful people did not write memorable poetry, but that I should not despair, for, like him, I was ugly enough to be a great poet.)

I know the night ended, but I'm not completely sure how. Once we got to John's room, he pleaded for a bottle of bourbon; room service was out. "They rob you," he announced, no doubt from considerable experience. He gave me a short list of his favorites, and I left him with Henri in attendance while he stretched out on his narrow bed, berating Coulette for letting him devour so many martinis and poisonous Scotch. "If my wife had been here, she would have managed me much better." I know I went out in search of a liquor store. Henri had drawn me a map and assured me it was only a few blocks away. Not trusting myself to drive, I decided to walk, but the streets curved and often suddenly ended, and before long I was completely lost. I searched my pockets, but the map was lost. I know I wandered helplessly for what seemed like hours and had no idea where I was. At one point I caught up with a woman carrying a small suitcase in hopes that she could point me the way to the Green Hotel. By this time the sky was turning gray, and I knew the dawn couldn't be far off. Unfortunately she didn't speak English, and at the time I knew no Spanish. We stood side by side at a traffic light at one of those wide LA boulevards with no traffic, I helpless and she on her way somewhere, perhaps to a job or a waiting family. She seemed for no reason I could fathom more than a little scared of me. I know by this time I was sober, and that somehow, an hour or so later—certainly by accident—I stumbled on the way to Coulette's apartment building, and there I found the state car where I'd left it the day before. It seemed pointless to awaken the Coulettes at five a.m. I chose to leave LA before the traffic got going and the freeways jammed up, and was back in Fresno in four hours, more than a little wrecked, and slept for much of that Saturday. I know that when I was myself again I didn't care if I ever saw John Berryman again, which was awful, since he was the finest teacher I'd ever had. I knew then a terrible truth that has remained with me to this day: love can die within me. The most brilliant man

I'd ever known was both going mad and killing himself, and I was stunned into an emotional silence. He was simply no longer the John Berryman I'd known, the generous teacher whose friendship I once valued as much as any I'd ever made, and I was no longer the young man who had adored him. My Berryman was gone, as was the Levine of 1954, and there was nothing I could think of to do about it.

•

I began this remembrance with the hope of presenting the Thom Gunn I knew for forty-five years, but having chosen to write about that particular day, I let Berryman dominate the narrative just as he had dominated the day. John could not *not* dominate the day; his demand for attention was epic, whereas Thom, who was so much less needy, could simply let the world come to him. John, when I knew him earlier, had his good days, but I had already seen him behave just as irrationally when drinking. He could be generous, kindly toward others, gentle, and in class he was always both brilliant and candid: somehow he seemed able to leave behind his madness. I believe he regarded teaching as a high calling, and he gave it his all, and he never compromised his beliefs to win the popularity or affection of his poetry students.

Thom was something else. Without the least effort on his part, he seemed larger than life. He was one of the half-dozen or so people I've known who had what I'll call an "aura," a sort of inner beauty that was manifest in all his actions. I doubt he was aware of how beautiful he was. Over the years he grew nobler—I know that's a ridiculous word to use in a contemporary context, but it seems right. His sweetness was overwhelming; each time I saw him over the years it was evident. I remember once in special in a restaurant in Berkeley, as I approached he got up, walked over to me, said "Phil" as though it were a charmed name, put his hands on my shoulders, and kissed me. He seemed totally unafraid to display his feelings. The first time he visited me in Fresno, I came back from some domestic chore to discover him in a rapt conversation with my three sons, the oldest of whom was twelve at the time. They were utterly relaxed in his presence and he in theirs, talking—of course—about contemporary pop music, which they were just discovering and about which he knew a surprising amount. No sooner had he left than they wanted to know when he was coming back. If Thom Gunn was who poets were, they were all for poets. Unfortunately he was not; never once in all the years did I ever hear him make a single reference to what we could call a "career" or complain that his work was not anthologized or revered. A much more typical remark from him was the following: He had just come back to California from England in the late sixties. "You won't believe this, Phil," he said, "they've discovered fun in England."

We took to exchanging books over the years, and we would comment on each other's work. I'll never forget one remark he made in a letter he sent me in '74 after he read my book *1933*. "Be careful, Phil," he wrote, "you are in danger of sentimentalizing the child you were." Such tact. I reread the book with his warning in mind, and saw that I had already done what I was in danger of doing. He also had a marvelous sense of humor and perfect timing. In the early sixties an editor at McGraw-Hill brought us together with the poet William Stafford to assemble a freshman reader for the enormous audience that hungered for it; we were promised a large advance and the certainty of a huge success. The meeting took place in a hotel suite in Berkeley after a huge, mediocre meal in the hotel dining

room. The editor, a big, sympathetic man you knew imme-
diately had failed at everything he'd tried, acted as though
he knew everything about selling books. He wanted each
of us to name pieces—essays, stories, poems—we thought
essential. Gunn and I seemed in accord: together we agreed
on a list that included Sartre's essays on American cities;
"America" by Allen Ginsberg; work by Henry Miller, Jean
Genet, Pierre Gascar, A. J. Liebling, Blake, James Baldwin,
Orwell, Rebecca West, Elizabeth Bishop, Paul Goodman,
Gary Snyder—writers we felt young people wouldn't oth-
erwise read and needed to read. We both wanted a reader
like no other. After enduring our proposals in silence for
twenty minutes, Stafford made it clear he could not put
his name on a reader that lacked Milton's "Areopagitica."
I remarked that the freshman students I taught at Fresno
State could never stay awake through the entire essay. The
editor had a great fondness for Stafford, but he saw imme-
diately we were not the right mix. Conversation flagged,
and soon Thom and I decided it was time for us to get back
to San Francisco, Thom to his apartment, me to the digs of
friends. As we stood waiting for the elevator, I said, "I really
like his poems." Meaning Stafford's, of course. "So do I,"
said Thom, and after a brief pause, "I wonder who writes
them."

A few years back he hosted two readings of August
Kleinzahler and me, the first on the campus of UC Berke-
ley, the second at Berkeley High. At the second, which took
place on a beautiful late morning in spring, Auggie and I
read to a small audience that was enclosed inside a much
larger audience made up of students who had no interest
in poetry. I was amazed by Thom's tact; he bargained with
these large, tough-looking young women: if they would
sit quietly in a corner at the back of this vast room and

speak softly and not giggle loudly as they removed their nail polish, he would not bring the wrath of their teachers and counselors down on them. As he arranged it, the event was a delight; we had about twenty-five kids directly in front of us who were taken with poetry, and in the background a sort of low tidal sound that disturbed no one. The hour ended with all of us satisfied. I thought then, Gunn is some sort of angel sent to earth to make us all feel better, and sometimes—when he was Thom Gunn the magnificent poet—to feel very deeply about our lives as well as the lives we didn't live or didn't comprehend until we lived inside his poems. I can't believe how much we've lost.

A MEANS OF TRANSPORT:
GEORGE HITCHCOCK
AND *kayak*

Aside from comic books, the first publication that obsessed me was *Life* magazine. I was probably only nine or ten when I discovered its riches, which were then available for a dime, a sum I could earn in an hour. No, it wasn't the politics or vision of Henry Luce, the booster of unrestrained capitalism, which grabbed me; the last thing I did was read the articles. It was the photographs: at first the war photographs from Spain and China and later those from Europe, North Africa, and the Pacific, as well as the great photographic record of an America stumbling through the blighted peace of the Depression with its breadlines, dust-bowl nightmares, and industrial cities going to ruin. Until I discovered the poetry of T. S. Eliot, the images of Robert Capa, Margaret Bourke-White, Dorothea Lange, Carl Mydans, Edward Clark, Alfred Eisenstaedt, and their colleagues were the most powerful I knew. When in high school I got into poetry, the word began to replace the photographic image, and by the time I came upon, at eighteen, "Preludes" by T. S. Eliot, the process was almost complete. Little wonder that two decades later I hit upon a magazine that fascinated me almost as much as *Life* had, and certainly more than any other literary publication. It was, of course, George Hitchcock's *kayak,* the first poetry journal I knew that was dedicated to the image and the only one I've ever ransacked with the same feverish anticipation I had those early issues of *Life.* In the very first issue, from a poet

I'd never heard of, Louis Z. Hammer, I stumbled across "Investigators are prying in the American bloodstream; / In Wyoming a horse dies by a silver river, / Two maiden sisters in Los Angeles have torn open their hands . . ." And from the editor himself:

> *America, beneath your promise*
> *there are underground lakes*
> *full of morphine and broken carburetors!*
>
> *Doors open and close on my shadow.*
> *My intestines burn. I am expelled*
> *from various academies.*

(The writing alone—even without the gas—would have gotten him expelled from any number of academies.) This was something new and different: it was neither the self-righteous rhetoric of the thirties protest poetry nor the overheated rant of the literary victim. Impossible to locate its origins in the American poetry of the forties and fifties or English poetry since the fall. This was a surrealism, or better an ultrarealism, whose fathers and mothers were unleashed Americans and whose uncles were Europeans, Iberians, and Latin Americans. There's a myth that American poetry was asleep during the Eisenhower years. American poetry has never been asleep; however, the best-known contemporary poetry during the postwar era was certainly powerfully sedated. The poets wild enough to be truly American were underground only because the official organs of reproduction were too sterile to allow them life anywhere else. What *kayak* did was collect these separate writers into a national movement and then sic them on the *Hudson* and *Sewanee Reviews.*

All you had to do was look at the magazine to know it was something new. (It's been copied so often that today someone first stumbling upon it might not recognize how striking it was in 1964.) Bound in heavy cardboard and voluminously illustrated, it sold for only a dollar, or three dollars for a two-year subscription of four issues. The paper itself had a crude substantiality—"target paper," I was later told, that George got cheaply. The illustrations were mainly engravings taken from odd and magical sources. For example, *kayak* 2 was dedicated to "America's Underground Channels and Seams," and the engravings were mainly taken from *Boston's Main Drainage* (1888) and André's *A Practical Treatise on Coal Mining* (1876). Each issue bore the following motto as an indication to possible contributors and readers of what the magazine's ambition was:

A kayak is not a galleon, ark, coracle or speedboat.
It is a small watertight vessel operated by a single
oarsman. It is submersible, has sharply pointed ends,
and is constructed from light poles and the skins
of furry animals. It has never yet been successfully
employed as a means of mass transport.

If you hoped to appear in the magazine, you had to paddle your own boat; where you were headed was your business. The epigones of Lowell and Wilbur were not welcome. From that first issue it was a place for me to discover new poets as well as a new vision of our poetry. It was here I first read John Haines, David Antin, Bert Meyers, Lou Lipsitz, Dennis Schmitz, Kathleen Fraser, Herbert Morris, Margaret Atwood, Charles Simic, Bill Knott, Margaret Randall, Adrien Stoutenburg, Shirley Kaufman, James Tate, Adam Cornford, Steve Dunn, Mark Doty, William Matthews,

Mark Jarman, and Brenda Hillman. Within a few issues well-known poets as diverse as Tom McGrath, David Ignatow, Louis Simpson, W. S. Merwin, John Logan, Wendell Berry, Hayden Carruth, Paul Blackburn, Donald Justice, Gary Snyder, Anne Sexton, Charles Wright, Raymond Carver, Stephen Dobyns, Charles Hanzlicek, Kenneth Rexroth, Peter Everwine, and Richard Hugo made appearances, and curiously none of them seemed in the wrong neighborhood: they sounded like themselves and like one of the voices of *kayak*. I can still recall Mark Strand telling me over thirty years ago, "I've got a poem coming out in *kayak*!" Clearly it had become the place to appear. I seriously doubt this was George's ambition for his eccentric journal, but for years the poets had been starved for just such a meeting space, and finding it we found it irresistible. I haven't mentioned translations, which became a regular feature of the magazine. Except for Rexroth's superb versions of the Chinese they were largely of twentieth-century European poets not yet discovered by many Americans: Rafael Alberti, Benjamin Peret, Odysseus Elytis, Vicente Huidobro, Hans Magnus Enzensberger, Tomas Tranströmer, et al.

By 1969 it had become a quarterly and was regularly publishing prose: not just prose poems, for they were there from the start, but prose prose—critical essays, reviews, and visionary opinion pieces representing utterly conflicting views. The reviews could be tough, sometimes even tough on regular *kayak* poets. (I was one who got bombed, although as I recollect not as badly as Dan Halpern in a review titled "Short Order Cooks of Poetry," which savaged Halpern's anthology of the younger American poets.) And the letters: one must not forget the letters, for they became for many a source of great wonder. An early one from Shirley Kaufman, a response to the Kayak Press book *Pioneers of Modern Poetry,* edited by George and Robert Peters, brought to our attention an all-but-unknown though masterful poet, Alexander Raphael Cury, whose poem "Inquiring About the Way," Kaufman demonstrated, had inspired Kafka, although the poem, unlike either *The Trial* or *The Castle,* ended on a note of hope:

> *I am going home.*
> > *Go home.*

> *What is the name of this place?*
> *Square*
> > *Street*
> > > *Lane.*

Equally delicious were the gripes. One from Rodney Nelson of San Francisco began:

> I hope you will excuse me for being direct: I see no
> point in sending *Kayak* any more poems or articles.
> The fact that you, as editor, are free to interpose
> your own personality between me and the readers
> is a sure indication that your magazine is socially
> unhealthy . . . Why should an editor steal a stamped,
> self-addressed envelope from a writer . . . Because
> nothing else matters but sly harassment, when the
> world is falling down around your ears. Into this picture
> fit you and your incredibly silly magazine, neither of
> which would last a minute in a people's society . . .

If this was the idiocy George was getting from the left, it's hard to imagine how much worse the complaints from the right were. From the start *kayak* presented found poems. I don't believe they were there only for laughs. The poets of that era—perhaps the poets of every era—had a tendency to exaggerate their social and spiritual significance. There was a lesson here for all of us who hoped to survive the violence and pain of the sixties: without a healthy and ribald disrespect for authority we were doomed. Like his great forebear Walt Whitman in the preface to *Leaves of Grass,* George was telling us in his own writing and in the sassy and irreverent entity that was *kayak* to take off our hats to no one.

I first met George Hitchcock in the spring of 1965. He'd come to Fresno as one of two poets reading on the Academy of American Poets California Circuit, which was then in its infancy. (Unfortunately it never lived into its teens.) The other poet was my old friend Henri Coulette. For the students at Fresno State it must have been something of an eye-opener; if they'd had any notions regarding the nature of the poet, his or her appearance, style, character, and writing, these two would have blown it. Henri was perhaps half a foot shorter than George and very slender—an ex–distance runner, he still looked as though he could do a mile in four minutes and change. He dressed in the style of an undersecretary of state on the threshold of a promotion: for day wear (and the reading took place in the early afternoon) he favored light-gray suits, bright ties, oxblood loafers. His dark hair was cut so short that its natural curliness was barely visible. His complexion was a light olive; he was, he claimed, in spite of his name a "black Irishman." George was a big man by any standard, and he carried himself with the exuberance of a very big man. Back in '65 he probably weighed a solid 230; his style of dress is hard to describe, for no extant term quite gets it. I'll call it post-Hemingway baroque. For daytime wear it could include anything from a foundry worker's coveralls to a purple tuxedo. His hair was just going gray and was so thick, long, and wild it looked as though it had never faced the shears of a trained barber. I thought immediately of Theodore Roethke during his greenhouse years.

Though both were superb readers, their styles had almost nothing in common. Coulette read from his wonderful first book, *The War of the Secret Agents,* with an almost icy precision that beautifully suited the work. Essentially a shy man, he spoke little between poems, which was a shame, for he possessed a fine sense of irony. Fortunately, it came through in the poems. Then it was George's turn. First he thanked Henri for the reading and for his companionship during their tour, and then he turned to his poems and opened up his enormous voice and let go. Nothing was more obvious than that he liked performing; he put his whole self into it. First his poems, serious and visionary, driven forward by the fury of his energy, original, surreal, and unpredictable:

> *I celebrate the swans with their invisible*
> *plumage of steam, I pursue fragrant bullets*
> *in the blue meadows, I observe in the reeds*
> *the sacraments of cellulose, I seek*
> *my lost ancestors.*

FROM "HOW MY LIFE IS SPENT"

He followed them with a short collection of riotously funny found poems: yes, this was truly the editor of what was becoming the most original and readable American poetry magazine in decades. I had asked myself before what was it that gave *kayak* such a potent and unified vision of the America of the sixties in spite of the fact it seemed to have room for almost every talented poet not writing Petrarchan sonnets (although George had published a wonderful parody of one), including many poets who couldn't even speak to each other: the answer was here in the character of George Hitchcock. Before the reading ended, George did something I have never seen another poet do: he turned to the audience and asked if there was anyone among us who would like to come forward and join the reading. No one took him up on it, so he turned to me and said, "Come on, Phil, you must have something to read!" I was so startled I declined the invitation. Generosity of this nature is not something one encounters very often on the reading trail, which is, unfortunately, where one is apt to see poets at their very worst, full of self and empty of a sense of others. George, I realized, was entirely sincere, and a word came into my mind that I have rarely brought to bear on anyone, much less a touring poet: bountiful. This guy had a lot to give, and the energy and character not to tire of giving it.

Everything I learned about George that first day I never unlearned, for he is exactly who he is: an adult in total possession of himself. There is no pose, no effort to charm—indeed he is naturally likable and charming—and his personality is so rich that every time I've been with him for a day or more I've been rewarded by new discoveries. The man who founded and edited for over a decade a truly great poetry journal had to be tough at times, had to possess high standards and his own vision of the poetry that mattered. As a nonacademic, he had no experience with committee decisions regarding artistic merit. George was a strong man with strong beliefs, one who was able to live with the dislike of others. (Have a look at his testimony before HUAC and you'll get an idea of what he thought of committee decisions and of courting dislike when it's worth treasuring.) You could say of George that what you see is what you get, but it wouldn't be true: you get more than you ever see.

Some years later George asked me if I'd like to do a book with Kayak Press. By this time he'd done books by Charles Simic and Raymond Carver, so the press—though a small one—was on the map of poetry. He warned me that it would be illustrated and that I would have no say in the matter as well as no say in the choice of the cover or in any aspect of the design. He wouldn't fool with the poems and I wouldn't fool with the production of the book, which was fine. I was by this time a devoted reader of the magazine as well as a delighted contributor, so I had a clear notion of just how eccentric his sense of illustration could be. I'd been having a terrible time finding a publisher for my third poetry collection. It had wandered from editor to editor collecting rejections. George had already printed the poem "They Feed They Lion" in *kayak,* but the manuscript of that title was sleeping in the editorial offices of Wesleyan University Press, where it would be awakened to a second rejection; but I had another collection, which I gave George. The submission and acceptance took place through the mail and required no contract or paperwork. I received a copy of the new book, *Red Dust,* a month ahead of schedule. It looked like no book I'd ever seen before, and I liked it. I even liked the poems; I hadn't had time to tire of them. In the letter that came with that first copy was a check which amounted to my royalties: he didn't want the trouble of screwing around with the bookkeeping, he was sure he'd sell all the copies, so here it was in dollars. That too never happened before or again. It may be a first in the history of poetry.

For many years I did not take George's poetry as seriously as it merited. I think I may have been so enraptured by his presence that I assumed that was the entrée of the feast he was. In 1984 he sent me a copy of a large collection, *The Wounded Alphabet*, which contains several extraordinary poems in his distinctive voice, poems as extraordinary as anything being written. Here is one, "End of Ambition," though I could have chosen "There's No Use Asking" or "His Last Words":

END OF AMBITION

*when I get there the last
mail has been sorted
my friends gather
in their arctic parkas
they speak a language
I don't understand
they've put off their
togas I don't recognize
the pumping station
or the grimy collier
docked at the pier*

*I'd waited a long time
I sat in the tower
for months weaving
these wings out of rage
and envy I'd almost
forgotten the song
of the parapets and
the green vision
we saw from the cliffs*

perhaps it's too late
perhaps they no longer
care the tide is out
the rules of flight
have been altered and
maybe there's no way now
to get beyond the clouds
of white corpuscles
and the tongues
darting and skimming
over the parched
mud-flats

To understate the matter, George gave the American poetry world three priceless gifts: his own writing; *kayak,* the finest poetry magazine of my era, and his complex and unusual presence, which served as a model for so many of us—the model of the poet as a total human being (as my mother would have said, a mensch). I've heard poets not a fraction as dedicated and gifted as George whine about how much they'd given America and how little it had given back. I've heard others literally cry for the lack of fame and fortune they'd suffered because they chose to be poets. I can't imagine anyone who'd been mentored by George, officially or otherwise, crying over his or her lack of celebrity. He or she would be much more likely to greet the closed door to fame with suitable defiance, and if words were required they'd likely be "Live free or die!" George was one of those Americans who spring up all too rarely, those originals who make you proud of your birthright: he loved this country so much he'd spent his life trying to make it a place worthy of its stated principles, its land and its people. Like anyone struggling to make his or her America a decent society,

George had known a history of losses; meeting him, you would never know it. His years in the labor movement had taught him all a person needs to know about loyalty, independence, and human dignity. His years as a gardener and an actor taught him the value of beauty and new growth. Those of us who shared his years as an editor and writer learned by example that a person can give his energy and heart to worthy ventures even in a corrupt society and never compromise. For those of us to whom he has been both mentor and friend—a huge portion of my generation of American poets—the gifts have been enormous, and no doubt different for each of us. I believe we all learned that the age-old conflict between art and life was nonsense: in George's case, nothing was more obvious than that art was his life and his life was an art. His laughter—like a totem against depression and defeat—I carry with me always, and his lesson that hard work in the service of a good cause is, like poetry, its own reward.

THE SPANISH CIVIL WAR
IN POETRY

I believe this obsession I have with Spain, her civil war, and especially the poetry of that war, has several sources from childhood and another from adulthood. At the age of seven I was told by my aunt, with whom I was living, that my father was of Spanish blood. She held up a photograph of him—he had been dead for two years—and explained that his olive skin, his dark eyes, and his long, slender face with its craggy features were Spanish. Of course I believed her. I later learned he was born in a village near Rovno in northern Ukraine, but of what use are facts to a child's imagination?

When I was seven my mother—who worked full-time—hired a hill woman from the Dakotas named Florence Hickok to cook, clean, and look after my twin brother and me during the summer. Florence was one of those uncompromising, totally authentic Americans who believe in decency, a fair wage, and a never-ending battle against the excesses of capitalism that all worthy working people were obliged by God and common sense to carry on until their last breath. Although she claimed "Wild Bill" Hickok as an ancestor, it was Tom Paine who was her spiritual father. Tall, gaunt, weatherbeaten, with a cigarette burning in the corner of her mouth, at the breakfast table five mornings a week she'd read through the *Free Press* muttering, "The bastards are selling us down the river." The bastards were the powerful, often invisible corporate giants who ran things in America and in Western Europe. By "us" she meant all those who had to work for a living, whose labor created the wealth that ironically shackled them. A year later, in the summer of '36, the generals rose up to overthrow the legally elected government of Spain. The three Detroit newspapers called it a battle between the Nationalists and the International Communist Conspiracy. From Florence I'd learned it was the people's government against the ancient repressive forces of church, army, and the great landowners and the new commercial barons. Hitler and Mussolini supported the Nationalists with arms and men, and Britain, France, and the United States (the so-called democracies) gave their tacit consent by refusing even to sell weapons to the Loyalists.

One Friday a year later, while loitering on the playing fields after school, my friend Irv told me his older brother, whose first name was the same as mine, was reported "missing in action" near the Ebro, a river I'd never heard of. That phrase, "missing in action," intrigued me, and I asked him what it meant. "He may be a prisoner of war," Irv said, "but my uncle says they aren't taking prisoners, so I guess it means he's dead." His tall, sturdy brother, Philip, was dead. The words haunted me: "Philip is dead." Of course, another, larger war would soon follow to devastate my family here and in Eastern Europe, but it was this Spanish war that pressed its imagery into my memory like no other, even the war of my generation, the Korean conflict, which cost me more personal grief.

Four years later, in the summer of '41, I took a job delivering dry cleaning on foot. I would often have to wait an hour or more while the work was completed. At first I would listen to the sermons of the Bulgarian tailor, a long-winded Communist theologian. After a month or so I switched my attention to the pants presser. In the intense heat he worked in pleated trousers that were themselves unpressed, and a sleeveless undershirt that revealed his scars, the result of his years of imprisonment for his loyalties to the Spanish anarchist cause. (Having forgotten his name, I've christened him Cipriano Mera, after another Spaniard whom he resembled.) A tightly built, muscular man with deep-set dark eyes and straight black hair, he went about his job with an alarming suddenness, as though he were not a pants presser at all but an actor playing the role of a pants presser. Within some months I began to read in his movements not a disregard for work but rather the affirmation that all work was worth doing with elegance and precision, and that useful work granted a share of dignity to the worker. His English was poor, his accent heavy, but I had no trouble following him when he told me of the necessary and unending struggle for equality and independence each of us must wage against the forces of government and private ownership. In spite of all his defeats he was animated by an amazing optimism. Pared of all excess, he seemed to me the perfect embodiment of the human spirit.

At twenty-five I was a college graduate, and an employee of General Motors for eight hours a night in the forge room of Chevy Gear & Axle at difficult, dangerous, and often stupefying work that week after week robbed me of whatever self-respect hadn't gone up in smoke. Florence and Cipriano had faded from my life, as had the notion of the dignity of labor. One Saturday afternoon in the stacks of the Wayne library I stumbled for the first time upon *Poet in New York*. I'd known García Lorca only as the author of "gypsy poems," a writer of lovely, exotic lyrics that meant little to me. When I opened this book and read

> *I denounce everyone*
> *who ignores the other half,*

the half that can't be redeemed,
who lift their mountains of cement
where the hearts beat
inside forgotten little animals
and where all of us will fall
in the last feast of pneumatic drills.
I spit in all your faces.

I knew I'd found my master. Never in poetry written in English had I found such a direct confrontation of one image with another or heard such violence enclosed in so perfect a musical form. What in my work had been a chaotic rant against American capitalism was in his a steady threnody circling around a center of riot. It took me another decade before I was able to realize his gift to me, which is not really that long if the result is a poem that means something to others. I know now that if I had not read

A wooden wind from the south, slanting through the
     black mire
spits on the broken boats and drives tacks into
     shoulders.
A south wind that carries
tusks, sunflowers, alphabets,
and a battery with drowned wasps

I could not have written

Out of burlap sacks, out of bearing butter
Out of black bean and wet slate bread,
Out of the acids of rage, the candor of tar,
Out of creosote, gasoline, drive shafts, wooden dollies,
They lion grow.

Lorca's book taught me that if I was able to remain true to my personal vision of this America, sooner or later poetry would come—certainly not poetry as amazing as Lorca's, but nonetheless poetry only I could write.

The little of modern Spanish poetry I knew, even in translation, thrilled me, and I was eager to encounter the country firsthand and learn what I could of its language, its poetry, and its civil war, but it was not until 1965 that I could afford to take my family. We settled in, of all places, Barcelona, which was then the Detroit of Iberia: industrial, polluted, unaware of its own beauties, and populated with an enraged working class with whom I felt utterly at home. In preparation I'd read or reread what I could find dealing with the civil war: the Hugh Thomas history, then the most inclusive in English; the poetry written by combatants and sympathizers; and Orwell's great memoir *Homage to Catalonia,* which begins with the following scene in the Lenin Barracks in Barcelona: It is December of '36, the anarchists are still in control of the city, and no one publicly says "señor" or "don" or even "usted," Orwell tells us. They say "Comrade"; instead of "Buenos dias" they say "Salud!" Tipping is forbidden. "Practically everyone wore rough working class clothes," Orwell wrote, "All this was queer and moving . . . but I recognized it immediately as a state of affairs worth fighting for," which he did. The day he enlisted in the militia he saw in the headquarters of the POUM an Italian militiaman: "His peaked leather cap was pulled fiercely over one eye . . . Something in his face deeply moved me. It was the face of a man who would commit murder and throw away his life for a friend—the kind of face you expect in an Anarchist . . ." For me it was the face of my old mentor Cipriano.

The poetry written by the English leftists of the thirties had in my student days inspired my work. Rereading it, I discovered that the most famous English poem of the war, Auden's "Spain," had nothing to do with military conflict and everything to do with the poet's struggle to accept or reject Marxism:

> *To-day the deliberate increase in the chances of death,*
> *The conscious acceptance of guilt in the necessary*
>   *murder,*
>   *To-day the expanding of powers*
> *On the flat ephemeral pamphlet and the boring*
>   *meeting.*
>
> *To-day the makeshift consolations: the shared cigarette,*
> *The cars in the candlelit barn, and the scraping concert,*
>   *The masculine jokes; to-day the*
> *Fumbled and unsatisfactory embrace before hurting.*
>
> *The stars are dead. The animals will not look.*
> *We are left alone with our day, and the time is short,*
>   *and*
>   *History to the defeated*
> *May say Alas but cannot help or pardon.*

This passage from the single poem he wrote about the war would not suggest Auden was committed to the defense of the Spanish Republic.

Of the others, it was Spender's that had once commanded the power to move me the most. For him this was a struggle for the survival of the Marxist ideal, but commitment does not always poetry make. Spender was essentially a romantic poet trying to expand his voice to encapsulate the horrors of modern war.

> *The guns spell money's ultimate reason*
> *In letters of lead on the spring hillside.*
> *But the boy lying dead under the olive trees*
> *Was too young and too silly*
> *To have been notable to their important eye.*
> *He was a better target for a kiss*
> . . . .
> *Consider his life which was valueless*
> *In terms of employment, hotel ledgers, news files.*
> *Consider. One bullet in ten thousand kills a man.*
> *Ask. Was so much expenditure justified*
> *On the death of one so young and so silly*
> *Lying under the olive trees, O world, O death?*

This is clearly about the evils of unrestricted capitalism; and as such it told me nothing I didn't know firsthand, and except for the olive trees nothing about Spain.

The combatants held up better. The two I recalled most clearly were Edwin Rolfe, the American Communist labor organizer who joined the Lincoln Brigade and served in Spain in 1937 and 1938, and the British Communist John Cornford who joined the POUM in 1936 and served on the Aragon front and later, as a member of the International Brigades, died in action on the Córdoba front one day after his twenty-first birthday. Much of Rolfe's war poetry dealt with combat he didn't take part in; he had enlisted to fight, but most of his assignments kept him away from the front and the poems show it.

CASUALTY

It seemed
the sky was a harbor, into which rode
black iron cruisers, silently, their guns
poised like tiger-heads on turret-haunches.

It seemed the sky was an olive grove, ghostly
in moonlight, and Very-light, with deadly crossfire
splitting it, proving a new theorem with rifles,
unknown in any recalled geometry.

And then he woke, choking. Saw sky as sky
in purest moonlight; and the searching beams paled
against it, and he heard Tibidábo's guns
burst against space. Then one bomb, shrieking,

found the thin axis of his whirling fears,
the exact center.

John Cornford had only a handful of poems to his credit when at the age of twenty he embarked for Spain. The son of an English poet and a classics professor, he came to literature early, and his essays on art, politics, and social justice attracted attention while he was in his teens. When I compare the following to Auden or Spender's war poems, I'm struck by the authority it gains from proximity to the actual as well as how contemporary it sounds.

A LETTER FROM ARAGON

This is a quiet sector of a quiet front.

We buried Ruiz in a new pine coffin,
But the shroud was too small and his washed feet
*   stuck out.*
The stink of his corpse came through the clean pine
*   boards*
And some of the bearers wrapped handkerchiefs
*   round their faces.*
Death was not dignified.
We hacked a ragged grave in the unfriendly earth
And fired a ragged volley over the grave.

Curiously, this sounds more American than Rolfe's. His most famous poem is this little one addressed to his beloved back in England:

Heart of the heartless world,
Dear heart, the thought of you
Is the pain at my side,
The shadow that chills my view.

The wind rises in the evening,
Reminds that autumn is near.
I am afraid to lose you,
I am afraid of my fear.

On the last mile to Huesca,
The last fence for our pride,
Think so kindly, dear, that I
Sense you at my side.

And if bad luck should lay my strength
Into the shallow grave,
Remember all the good you can;
Don't forget my love.

Except for the reference to Huesca, it could be a poem about any war.

Settled in a village on the outskirts of Barcelona, I had the good luck to encounter two poets who became my mentors. The first was Hardie St. Martin, the editor of *Roots and Wings,* an anthology of Spanish poetry translated by American poets. He invited me to join the project. The other, the Catalan poet Joan Rusinyol, my conversational-Spanish teacher, discovered I was a poet and managed to conduct half the lessons in English so I could discuss with him the subtleties of Whitman and Robinson Jeffers, two of his great passions, and he could lecture me on Unamuno, Antonio Machado, and Juan Ramón. Before long I took the plunge and began translating, at first badly, Spanish and Latin American poetry—poems which were to become a constant source of inspiration as well as a continuing lesson in humility. I began with Rafael Alberti, from his great book *Sobre los ángeles,* which I got all wrong, since I thought the title meant "Above the Angels" rather than "About Angels." I did *not* translate this poem about the death of García Lorca; it was already beautifully done by Mark Strand:

THE COMING BACK OF AN ASSASSINATED POET

You have come back to me older and sadder in the
drowsy
light of a quiet dream in March, your dusty temples

disarmingly gray, and that olive
bronze you had in your magical youth,
furrowed by the passing of years, just as if
you lived out slowly in death
the life you never had while you were alive.

I do not know what you wanted to tell me tonight
with your unexpected visit, the fine alpaca
suit, looking like new, the yellow tie,
and your carefully combed hair
suffering the wind the same as when
you walked through those gardens of poplars
and hot oleanders of our school days.

Maybe you thought—I want to explain myself
now that I stand outside the dream—that you
had to come first to me from those buried
roots or hidden springs where
your bones despair.
                    Tell me,
tell me,
if in the mute embrace you have given me,
in the tender gesture of offering me a chair, in the
        simple
manner of sitting near me, of looking at me,
smiling and in silence, without a single word,
tell me if you did not mean
that in spite of our minor disagreements,
you remain joined to me more than ever in death
for the time perhaps
we were not—oh, forgive me!—in life.

If this is not true, come back again in a dream
some other night to tell me so.

It struck me that if Alberti could in his imagination rein-
vent the dead poet to heal the rift between them, I could
enter the Spain of 1937 to witness the loss of my schoolmate's
brother, and like the great Spanish poet I could address my
lost friend directly as though he could hear.

TO P.L., 1916–1937

a soldier of the Republic

Gray earth peeping through snow,
you lay for three days
with one side of your face
frozen to the ground. They tied your cheek
with the red and black scarf
of the Anarchists, and bundled you
in canvas, and threw you away.
Before that an old country woman
of the Aragon, spitting on her thumb,
rubbing it against her forefinger,
stole your black Wellingtons,
the gray hunting socks, and the long
slender knife you wore
in a little leather scabbard
riding your right hip. She honed it,
ran her finger down the blade, and laughed,
though she had no meat to cut,
blessing your tight fists
that had fallen side by side
like frozen faces on your hard belly
that was becoming earth. (Years later
she saw the two faces

at table, and turned from the bread
and the steaming oily soup, turned
to the darkness of the open door,
and opened her eyes to darkness
that they might be filled with anything
but those two faces squeezed
in the blue of snow and snow and snow.)
She blessed your feet, still pink,
with hard yellow shields of skin
at heel and toe, and she laughed
scampering across the road, into
the goat field, and up the long hill,
the boots bundled in her skirts,
and the gray hunting socks, and the knife.
For seven weeks she wore the boots
stuffed with rags at toe and heel.
She thought she understood
why you lay down to rest
even in snow, and gave them to a nephew,
and the gray socks too.
The knife is still used, the black handle
almost white, the blade
worn thin since there is meat to cut.
Without laughter she is gone
ten years now,
and on the road to Huesca in spring
there is no one to look for you
among the wild jonquils, the curling
grasses at the road side,
and the blood red poppies, no one
to look on the farthest tip
of wind breathing down from the mountains
and shaking the stunted pines you hid among.

Of all the poets I read during those years, the one who remains most vividly with me is Antonio Machado. Nothing in his work is flashy or hurried, the details are common, the vocabulary modest, the poet's stance never heroic or even dramatic. A typical Machado poem walks us down a country road or through a sleeping village or out into the orchards to observe what is timeless: dawn or dusk or the transformations of sunlight or moonlight.

OVER COARSE STONE IN THE MIDDLE OF THE SQUARE

Over coarse stone in the middle of the square
water drips and drips. In the nearby grove a tall
cypress tree, and behind an ivy-draping wall
rises a stain of rigid branches in the air.

The afternoon is falling into dreams, a lull
before the large houses in the plaza. Window glare
with macabre echoes of the sun, and forms stare
from balconies and fade like blurring skulls.

Across the barren plaza infinite calm abounds
where the soul trails the outline of a tortured soul.
Water drips and drips in the marble bowl.
In all the air in shadow only water sounds.

The war was a catastrophe for Machado. Because he'd remained loyal to the Republic, he was separated from those he was closest to. The violent emotions the war generated in Spaniards prodded him into a kind of poetry he had avoided. In his lament for García Lorca we can hear in the repetitions, the striking figures, and the diction echoes of Lorca's own work.

THE CRIME WAS IN GRANADA

1. The Crime

He was seen walking between rifles
down a long street
and going out to the cold countryside
with stars of early dawn.
They killed Federico
when light came.
The squad of executioners
didn't dare look him in the face.
They all closed their eyes.
They prayed, "Not God can save you!"
Dead fell Federico
—blood on his forehead and lead in his stomach—.
That the crime was in Granada—
know it!—Poor Granada!—in his Granada!

2. The Poet and Death

He was seen walking alone with her,
not afraid of her scythe.
—The sun already on tower and tower; the hammers
on the anvil—anvil and anvil of forges.
Federico was speaking,
flirting with death. She listened.
"Companion, because yesterday in my verse,
the clapping of your dry palms resounded

and you gave ice to my song, and edge
of your sickle of silver to my tragedy,
I will sing you your missing flesh,
the eyes you lack,
your hair the wind was ruffling,
the red lips where they kissed you . . .
Today as before, gypsy, my death,
how good it is alone with you
in these breezes of Granada, my Granada!"

3.

He was seen walking . . .
        Friends, carve
a tomb of stone and dream in the Alhambra,
for the poet,
over a fountain where the water weeps
and forever says,
The crime was in Granada, in his Granada!

Lorca was thirty-eight years old, at the very height of his powers as a playwright and poet, when in August of 1936 he was taken by local fascists to a hillside near his home and—as we say today—disappeared, a death which has haunted Spain and poetry ever since and lies at the center of dozens of poems, including many American poems. Having seen the extraordinary improvement in public education and human rights under the Republic, both Lorca and Machado felt a powerful emotional investment in the cause. Before Valencia was cut off from the Loyalist forces, Machado made it to Barcelona, and when the Republican forces collapsed he, along with the ragged remains of the army and those with good reason to fear the retributions exacted upon the defeated, crossed into France in the winter of 1939. Shortly thereafter he died, it is said, of a broken heart, and was buried in Spanish earth.

The great Peruvian poet César Vallejo, a committed Marxist, after a six-month imprisonment left his native country for good. From 1923 until 1930, when he was expelled for political reasons, he lived in France, where he and his wife existed very poorly on his income as a writer. He then moved to Madrid, where he didn't do much better, writing stories and articles for magazines and his only novel, *Tungsteno*. He was back in Paris in 1932, and then when, four years later, the civil war broke out, he returned to Spain to do what he could in defense of the Republic. There he wrote some of his most powerful poetry, much of which was first printed by Loyalist militias. Suffering from a strange, never-diagnosed malady, he was rushed back to Paris, where he died on Good Friday, April 15, 1938. What follows is an example of his poetry that arose out of the revolution and the civil war.

WITH HIS INDEX FINGER
HE USED TO WRITE
ON THE AIR . . .

With his index finger he used to write on the air:
"Long live the comrades! Pedro Rojas."
Of Miranda del Ebro, father and man,
husband and man, rail worker and man,
father—but even more man—Pedro and his two
    deaths.

A wind-borne scrap of paper, they killed him (this
  really happened)
A feather of flesh and blood, they killed him!
Go tell all the comrades at once!

A pole on which they hung their beam,
they killed him;
they killed him to the base of his forefinger!
At one and the same time they killed both Pedro and
  Rojas!

Long live the comrades
on the honor roll of the air!
May they live long with the V of the vulture in the
  guts
of Pedro
and of Rojas, hero and martyr!

Searching him after death, they surprised
within his body a body big enough to hold
the soul of the world,
and in his pocket an empty spoon.

Pedro also had the habit of eating
with the members of his family, of embellishing
his table and living pleasantly
like anyone else,
and that spoon stayed always in his jacket,
awake or asleep, always
that dead-alive spoon, with its symbolic meaning.
Inform all the comrades at once!
Let them bow before this spoon forever.

They killed him, forced death on him,
on Pedro, on Rojas, on the worker, the man, the one
who was once such a little baby, who looked at the
> *sky,*
and later grew up and became a Red,
struggling with every cell of his body, with his yeas
> *and nays,*
> *his doubts, his hungers and the pieces of himself.*

They killed him with finesse
amid the tresses of his wife, Juana Vásquez,
in the hour of fire, the year of the bullet,
and just when he was getting at the meaning of
> *things.*
Pedro Rojas, after his death,
raised himself up, kissed his bloody catafalque,
wept for Spain,
and once again wrote with his finger on the air:
"Long live the comrades! Pedro Rojas."

His dead body contains all the world

TRANSLATED BY
LILLIAN LOWENFELS AND NAN BRAYMER

Pedro Rojas—like Cipriano Mera—is committed to a
revolutionary cause, though unlike Cipriano he struggles
with his "nays," his doubts; as husband and father as well
as worker, he has much more to lose, and of course he loses
it all. In his photographs Vallejo bore a strong resemblance
to Cipriano—spare, essential, shabbily dressed. Like Cipri-
ano, he was intellectually ferocious: they were two serious

men obsessed with the need for radical change. Perhaps Whitman also sponsored my poem when in his introduction to *Leaves of Grass* he advised the American poet to go among powerful, uneducated people and take off his hat to no one.

TO CIPRIANO, IN THE WIND

Where did your words go,
Cipriano, spoken to me 38 years
ago in the back of Peerless Cleaners,
where raised on a little wooden platform
you bowed to the hissing press
and under the glaring bulb the scars
across your shoulders—"a gift
of my country"—gleamed like old wood.
"Dignidad," you said into my boy's
wide eyes, "without is no riches."
And Ferrente, the dapper Sicilian
coatmaker, laughed. What could
a pants presser know of dignity?
That was the winter of '41, it
would take my brother off to war,
where you had come from, it would
bring great snowfalls, graying
in the streets, and the news of death
racing through the halls of my school.
I was growing. Soon I would be
your height, and you'd tell me
eye to eye, "Someday the world
is ours, some day you will see."
And your eyes burned in your fine

*white face until I thought you
would burn. That was the winter
of '41, Bataan would fall
to the Japanese and Sam Baghosian
would make the long march
with bayonet wounds in both legs,
and somehow in spite of burning acids
splashed across his chest and the acids
of his own anger rising toward his heart
he would return to us and eat
the stale bread of victory. Cipriano,
do you remember what followed
the worst snow? It rained all night
and in the dawn the streets gleamed,
and within a week wild phlox leaped
in the open fields. I told you
our word for it, "Spring," and you said,
"Spring, spring, it always come after."
Soon the Germans rolled east
into Russia and my cousins died. I
walked alone in the warm spring winds
of evening and said, "Dignity." I said
your words, Cipriano, into the winds.
I said, "Someday this will all be ours."
Come back, Cipriano Mera, step
out of the wind and dressed in the robe
of your pain tell me again that this
world will be ours. Enter my dreams
of my life, Cipriano, come back
out of the wind.*

The war was an epic experience for Pablo Neruda, who was living in Spain attached to the Chilean consulate when it began. His poems (along with those of Alberti and Hernández), he tells us in his autobiography, were printed and then carried into battle by the militiamen. It was in Spain he became a dedicated Communist and a poet committed to the welfare of all working people. His response to the fascist uprising was his enraged book *Spain in Our Hearts*. These are two of its calmer poems:

MOLA IN HELL

The turbid Mola mule is dragged
from cliff to eternal cliff
and as the shipwrecked man goes from wave to wave,
destroyed by brimstone and horn,
boiled in lime and gall and deceit,
already expected in hell,
the infernal mulatto goes, the Mola mule
definitively turbid and tender,
with flames on his tail and his rump.

THE UNIONS AT THE FRONT

Where are the miners? Where are
the rope makers, the leather
curers, those who cast the nets?
Where are they?

Where are those who used to sing at the top
of the building, spitting and swearing
upon the lofty cement?

Where are the railroadmen
dedicated and nocturnal?
Where is the supplier's union?

With a rifle, with a rifle. Among the
dark throbbing of the plainland,
looking out over the debris.

Aiming the bullet at the harsh
enemy as at the thorns,
as at the vipers, that's it.

By day and by night, in the sad
ash of dawn, in the virtue
of the scorched noon.

Poems came from everywhere. Let me name a few of the writers I especially admire, and one I detest: from England, Christopher Caudwell, Julian Bell, and Ralph Fox, all of whom died in combat; from France, Aragon and Éluard; from the USA, Langston Hughes, Muriel Rukeyser, Kenneth Rexroth, and Kenneth Fearing; from exile, Bertold Brecht; from Spain and Latin America, León Felipe, Manuel Altolaguirre, Luis Cernuda, Jorge Guillén, and the Nobelist-to-be Vicente Aleixandre; from Scotland, the great Communist poet Hugh MacDiarmid; and from South Africa, the vitriolic fascist Roy Campbell. Catalunya alone sponsored five thousand new poets published by local communes, poets who recognized themselves as the real thing, since they were entirely self-taught. For the progressive citizens of the world, the period of the civil war was an extraordinary confluence of people of goodwill and artistic gifts committed to the struggle against the old forces of pietism, reaction, racism, and the abuses of ownership and power. Sixty years have passed and you and I have seen nothing like it again. Little wonder a portion of so many of us still lives in 1936 and searches among the ruins of the lost Spanish war for that singular unity.

I'll end this address by reading three poems. First, "How Much for Spain," by Michael Quinn, which appeared in the *Daily Worker* in 1937. I found it only a few months ago in Cary Nelson's book *Revolutionary Memory*.

HOW MUCH FOR SPAIN?

The long collection speech is done
And now the felt hat goes
From hand to hand its solemn way
Along the restless rows.
In purse and pocket, fingers feel
And count the coins by touch.
Minds ponder what they can afford
And hesitate . . . how much?
In that brief, jostled moment when
The battered hat arrives,
Try, brother, to remember that
Some men put in their lives.

The poem that follows is one that always reaffirms my belief in the human spirit and the value of poetry. I can't imagine a more useful poem. Its author, Miguel Hernández, was born in the village of Orihuela, inland from Alicante. As a young goatherd he educated himself in the local school and the church libraries. Meeting him in Madrid just before the outbreak of war, Neruda wrote that he had the face of a potato just pulled from the earth. His writing developed at an astonishing pace, and by age twenty-one he had found his unique voice, a combination of the formally elegant and the surreal, work so intense and startling it immediately caught the attention of his fellow poets. In the late poetry a folkloric element enters, the tight formalism relaxes, and he gives us a poetry of enormous authenticity and power. García Lorca, in a letter written to him after the publication of his first book, predicted a glorious literary future. It was not to be. A believer in the rights of the individual, he enlisted in the Republican army. His work, too, was printed by the Loyalist militias and actually carried into battle by countless soldiers. When the war ended he was a marked man; lacking the right documents, he was denied entry into Portugal, Spain's fascist neighbor to the west. Imprisoned, in less than three years he developed tuberculosis and died at age thirty-two. This poem, "Lullabies of the Onion," was sent from prison to his wife after she had written him that she had nothing to feed their young son except bread and onions, the apples of the poor.

LULLABIES OF THE ONION

The onion is frost
shut in and poor.
Frost of your days
and of my nights.
Hunger and onion,
black ice and frost
large and round.

My little boy was
in hunger's cradle.
He suckled on
onion blood.
But your blood is
frosted with sugar,
onion and hunger.

A dark woman dissolved
into moonlight
spills, thread by thread,
over the cradle.
Laugh, child,
you can drink moonlight
if you have to.

Lark of my house,
laugh freely.
Your laughter in your eyes
is the world's light.
Laugh so much
that hearing you, my soul
will beat through space.

Your laughter frees me,
gives me wings.
It banishes loneliness,
tears down these walls.
Mouth that flies,
heart that flashes
on your lips.

Your laughter is
the supreme sword,
conqueror of flowers
and larks.
Rival of the sun.
Future of my bones
and of my love.

The flesh flutters
as sudden as an eyelid;
life, as never before,
takes on new color.
How many linnets,
wings beating, take off
from your body!

I woke from childhood:
don't you ever.
I wear my mouth sadly:
always laugh.
Stay always in your cradle
defending laughter
feather by feather.

You are a flight
so high, so wide,
that your flesh is heaven
just born.
If only I could climb
to the origin
of your flight!

In the eighth month you laugh
with five orange blossoms.
With five little
ferocities,
with five teeth
like five young
jasmine buds.

They will be the frontier
of kisses tomorrow
when you feel a gun
in your mouth.
When you feel a burning
past the teeth
searching for the center.

Fly, child, on the double moon
of her breast:
it is saddened by onions,
you are satisfied.
Never let go.
Don't ever know what's coming,
what goes on.

TRANSLATED BY PHILIP LEVINE

In the fall of 1965 some of Spain's most honored poets, critics, and scholars decided to convene in Orihuela, where his wife and son still lived, to pay homage to Hernández. Although this was close to thirty years after the end of the war, the Franco government had softened not at all, and all those bound for the conference were turned back by the Guardia Civil. This non-event, which I did not take part in, stuck in my memory and fermented. I, who have always believed in the possibility of the return of the dead, wrote this little poem thirty-some years later after imagining the great poet's return. It is foolhardy to close with my work after the great poems from Spain, but so be it.

THE RETURN: ORIHUELA, 1965

for Miguel Hernández

You come over a slight rise
in the narrow winding road
and the white village broods
in the valley below. A breeze
silvers the cold leaves
of the olives, just as you knew
it would or as you saw
it in dreams. How many days
have you waited for this day?
Soon you must face a son grown
to manhood, a wife to old age,
the tiny sealed house of memory.
A lone crow drops into the sun,
the fields whisper their courage.

IN THE NEXT WORLD:
THE POETRY
OF ROBERTA SPEAR

When Roberta Spear died of leukemia in the spring of 2003, she left behind not only a grieving family, but also an almost-completed fourth book of poems. Thirty years earlier, when her husband was assigned to a hospital in Fresno to do his residency, she'd returned from Winston-Salem, North Carolina, where he had studied medicine and she had taught creative writing at Wake Forest. Thus she was back in the Central Valley, where she'd grown up in the town of Hanford, some thirty miles south of Fresno. Only now she was not only a poet but also the mother of a son and soon a daughter. For as long as she lived she gave herself totally to the roles of wife, mother, poet, and friend to the cluster of poets settled in and around Fresno. California's Central Valley is one of the keys to her poetry, for above all else Roberta was a poet of "person, place, and thing." The people of central California are the people of more than half her poems; the landscape and the climate of scorching summers and fog-bound winters appear and disappear in these poems. The Valley, as it's known here, is not the California of the movies, unless the movie you have in mind is *The Grapes of Wrath*, for it is exactly the place to which the Joads arrive on their trek from Oklahoma with all their hopes for a better life soon to go unfulfilled. In Hanford she would have grown up with the children of the Joads or people like them who shared that journey, as well as with the children of farmers and ranchers and the Chicanos and African-Americans who worked in their fields, orchards, and vineyards. And she would have watched with them as the years brought smog, chronic unemployment, and gang warfare. Once it may have been the rural idyll described by John Muir when he first crossed the Pacheco Pass and beheld it from the north. Now it is twenty-first-century America, the small towns bursting with the new immigrants from Southeast Asia and the American rust belt.

How could a poet find so much to sing about in a place like this, for sing is what she did? From her poem "Two Trees":

> *And from the kitchen table,*
> *I can see the shadows shift*
> *as the pecan breathes in the sunlight.*
> *I wonder if this giant,*
> *the grandfather of our back field,*
> *still has what it takes*
> *under these tendons of bark,*
> *the layers riddled by seasons of birds,*
> *or if the young dogwood tipped with green*
> *will surprise us next March.*

There are two crucial words in that passage: "wonder" and "surprise." By some amazing alchemy Spear seemed able to waken each day—or at least each day that's recorded in her poetry—with a sense of wonder in the presence of the physical world, as though each dawn were a surprise, an event like none other in the history of experience. There is a kind of primal innocence in her poetry; she sees a world untainted by the brutal forces that have turned the Valley into an ongoing catastrophe. It's not that she was unaware or ignorant of what was around her; it's simply that the present with all its riches, with all the majesty of its being tangible, was amazing to her, a gift, each moment a moment of miraculous potential, and she saw her function as a poet to observe it, to detail it, to name it, and when all her forces as an artist were at her command, to bless it. And those forces were hers more often than not. The answer to the question that began this paragraph—how could she sing?—is mysterious, and has much to do with her sense of fulfillment as a woman as well as the glory of her individual being. She was always a creature of hope. In all the years I knew her, I never knew her to despair.

And I knew her for thirty-four years, since she was a very young woman enrolled in an advanced class in poetry writing at Fresno State, a class that someone had let swell to forty students. That first evening the class met, in a cavernous, unadorned chemistry lab that appalled me, I behaved very badly on purpose, for I was determined to get it down to something manageable and to move the smaller class to a more intimate setting, and to do so I set about terrifying the students. Each week, I told them, they'd be required to hand in a new poem in whatever form I required: for example, thirty lines of anapestic tetrameter without an adjective. Perhaps twenty heroic couplets in the style of Charles Churchill, or a blank-verse monologue in the voice of Henry Ford on the theme of the Jews. When I paused to take a breath, a fresh young blonde woman asked if I recognized free verse. I said that I did, and that I'd seen a lot of it of late. She informed me that in Galway Kinnell's class at UC Irvine the students decided what forms they wrote in. I mused for a moment and replied that it was an interesting notion. Kinnell was certainly a marvelous poet, who, I noted, had written brilliantly in traditional

forms early in his writing life. It worked: the next week only
sixteen students showed up; the others had dropped out.
And the blonde? She was, of course, Roberta Spear. Kinnell
had advised her to come to Fresno if she was serious about
becoming a poet, and she was not about to be discouraged
by my folderol. As the weeks passed, I began to discover her
poems and also to discover the iron-willed person who had
written them.

A few years later she enrolled in a translation class I taught
with the Spanish-born critic and scholar Jose Elgorriaga,
and I believe it was there that she discovered the poetry of
Rafael Alberti, Gloria Fuertes, and Pablo Neruda. She loved
the sharp tongue and quick wit of Fuertes's poems, that
talking back to men of prestige and power and the whole
rigged system that was Franco's Spain, in which an ordinary
working woman might drown without anyone noticing.
But for her Neruda was supreme—a poet the likes of whom
she had never before encountered—for it was in his work,
her friend Sandra Hoben writes, that she found "the differ-
ence between most poetry and what the greats were up to."
His *Odas Elementales* were especially significant, for it was
in them that the great Chilean honors the things of every
day—a suit, a pinch of salt, an onion, a pair of socks, the
color green—so as to create an event of cosmic significance,
and he does it with wit, style, at times an almost preposter-
ous vocabulary, and always with a smile. After Neruda her
aims in poetry were never the same; she now had a stan-
dard, a far clearer notion of "the poem" she was after.

At a time when so many young women poets were dis-
covering and bathing in the river that was Plath, Spear was
almost totally uninterested: she wrote that she resented "the
common association between the woman poet, neurosis,
and kitchen sinks." In fact she was far more interested in

the poetry of Ted Hughes, with its extraordinary evocations of beasts and men and the pure energy that drives his lyrics forward toward an apocalyptic moment. Not that she ever tried to imitate his raucous, grinding music or ever accepted his vision of the eternal war among all creatures; the music of her poetry is far quieter and more adapted to her own vision, in which the individual often merges with the *other*. In terms of the music of her poetry, D. H. Lawrence, especially in his superb Rhine Valley poems, was truly influential. Her poetry arrived, she wrote, "especially when [I was] overwhelmed by the pure physicalness of myself, other people, or my surroundings." In a singular way she envisioned herself as another aspect of her environment, the one gifted with the language to speak for all the individual creations that made up her world. That Nerudaesque urge to blend with all things and to give all things their voice you can hear swelling in many of her finest poems.

> *Yet, a few things explained*
> *by all this racket. Life must be named,*
> *called back often before it wanders too far.*
> *And so, a mother lifts her skirt*
> *and slowly wades into the water*
> *after a child who would rather follow*
> *the fish to their smoky depths.*
> *Also, there are always those*
> *who mean nothing when they speak,*
> *who, like birds, love the sound of air so much*
> *they wave their arms, their tongues*
> *and give it away.*

FROM "CINQUE TERRE:
THE LAND OF FIVE NOISES"

One reviewer of her first book (Robert Peters in the *American Book Review*) wrote of her "quiet, hard-seeing way of moving at, into, and through natural objects, assimilating them into her vision." Another (Joseph Parisi in the *Chicago Tribune*) praised her gift for metaphor and imagery that suggest "the mysterious depths beneath her shining surfaces." In a prose statement in the anthology *What Will Suffice* she illuminates the source of her poem "Diving for Atlantis":

> At the time I wrote "Diving for Atlantis," I was pregnant with my first child and living in the South (North Carolina). The world around me seemed unbelievably vibrant and intriguing. The children who swam around me at the local "Y" demonstrated what I had already learned as a poet—that the imagination has an infinite capacity for transforming one's identity and surroundings . . . Just as the children dive into the water to look for the mythical city of Atlantis, the poet must penetrate the layers of the imagination until the vision is realized.

Writing of her final book, *The Pilgrim Among Us,* the poet Edward Hirsch described her as a poet who "transfigures the ordinary and pinpoints the mysteries of daily life . . ." And Margaret Gibson, commenting on the same book, wrote that in Spear's poetry "it's the ordinary which is discovered to be the site of the extraordinary." Anyone who reads her will be struck by her ability to focus her attention on that which often seems beneath our attention, and find there the source of her own visionary poems. One of her favorite poems was "Grappa in September" by the great Italian poet Cesare Pavese, which she read both in the Italian and in the translation of William Arrowsmith. It is not a typical Pavese poem; Pavese in the poems of *Hard Labor* is most often a narrative poet, but in this poem nothing happens. The poem is merely a description of a northern Italian village at the end of summer. We discover the house at the field's edge that sells tobacco "which is blackish in color / and tastes of sugar . . . / They also have grappa there, the color of water." The final stanza begins:

> *This is the time when every man should stand*
> *still in the street and see how everything ripens.*

If Spear saw this poem as a metaphor for her own work I do not know, but I do know that she read it over and over, and that she found in it an almost mystical sense of what the poetry she loved was capable of. I know also that she was much taken with a remark of Pavese's from his book on American literature: "The new symbolism of Whitman meant, not the allegorical structures of Dante but a . . . sort of double vision through which, from the single object of the senses vividly absorbed and possessed, there radiates a sort of halo of unexpected spirituality." It was of course that aspect of American poetry, which she found first in Whitman, Williams, and Stevens especially and later in the contemporaries she most valued, that she worked to incorporate in her own work.

•

Rereading her poetry, I cannot hear the least suggestion of a familiarity with my poetry or the poetry of her first poetry-writing teacher, Galway Kinnell, but one teacher had a profound effect on the voice she created for herself or the voice that found her in her mature poems, and that was the voice of Peter Everwine. She had already studied Antonio Machado and Juan Ramón Jiménez and admired the crystalline quality and the precision that is the hallmark of their work. She caught echoes of something similar in those delicate love poems of Lawrence, but the first time she encountered it in an American voice was in Everwine's work. Here is that voice in a poem from his second book, *Keeping the Night*, "Perosa Canavese," written shortly after his first trip to the village of his ancestors:

> *What I came for*
> *—all those miles—*
> *was to see the face of the village*
> *my people spoke of*
> *in the hour before sleep,*
> *and which I was given for my own*
> *like an empty locket,*
> *like a mirror in a locked room.*

In a poem from her first book called "The Traveler," dedicated to Everwine, she answers him in that new voice that will become the voice of much of her poetry.

> *At the edge of the village,*
> *battered stalks and then a field*
> *of poppies. You drop your pack*
> *to the ground, picking*
> *the few that will last*
> *until you find others.*
> *Among the stalks,*
> *an old farmer*
> *whose plow has died.*

> *Wearing these flowers*
> *you remind him of his son*
> *who let the fields*
> *go to seed. Not everyone*
> *will be quick to claim you . . .*

This was written after her second trip to Italy in 1979, and it constitutes the first poem in an extended conversation with her former teacher.

Her first trip to Italy, in 1967, and especially the second, in '79, were of momentous importance in her development as a person and a poet. She literally fell in love with the people and the landscape, and they appear in many of the poems that were to follow. (She would return to Italy two more times, the last time in 2000 with her son and daughter.) She also fell in love with the language, to which she devoted years of study so that she might read the poets whose language it was—from Dante to Ungaretti, Pavese, and Sinisgalli—and occasionally translate them. Much as she admired Everwine's voice and his strategies, there was in Spear a natural volubility, a sense of luxury and abundance that was absent in Everwine's work. His line suited her perfectly and she retained it for the rest of her career, but his rigorous sense of economy, the total absence of the baroque in his writing, that urge that her earlier love and study of Neruda's odes had nurtured, couldn't find room to expand and play unless she let go. This created a tension that the poems themselves exploited, for Roberta's poems had the habit of seeking a larger, more expansive format, and she had the good sense to let them. She also had a strong sense of narrative; she wanted to tell in verse the family stories she inherited—to become, as it were, the family mythmaker. Indeed, she found stories everywhere, but like her beloved

Pavese she found them mostly in the ordinary people who inhabited the various neighborhoods that had been or were to become home. And since home for the last three decades of her life was Fresno, they frequently became the stories of American immigrants, especially those from Asia and Mexico. You could say at times she saw stories where there were none or where she simply invented them, exotic stories of gypsies and pranksters, travelers and seekers, those with whom she identified. This is most obvious in what is for me her finest book, *Taking to Water,* which is truly a volume of magic, one that transforms the ordinary things of daily life into tales to conjure with, as in the conclusion of "Map for the Unborn":

> *Follow the line that runs*
> *from the thumb to the heart*
> *until lines cover your face*
> *and your legs give in.*
> *Circle the mound of your smallest finger*
> *twice around the world*
> *until your fortune comes and goes*
> *and a villager opens his window*
> *to call you inside.*
> *He will take your hand*
> *and ask to hear your stories,*
> *for you have crossed the seas*
> *of your mother, and who can remember*
> *having traveled so far?*

In the last years of her life she found new works to admire, poets she hadn't known, and with her usual generosity of spirit she touted them (I'm thinking especially of the late books of Larry Levis and Ruth Stone and *New Addresses* by

Kenneth Koch and *Time and Money* by William Matthews) more than she pushed her own work. The discovery of a true poet that mattered was an extraordinary event for her; Zbigniew Herbert, Miłosz, Szymborska, Sabines, Nancy Willard, she came back to again and again. On several occasions I loaded her down with the books I'd received in the mail, and her joy at what treasures they might hold was lovely to behold. In truth she never pushed her own work. She decided early on and after only a few experiences that she disliked giving poetry readings; and although she knew this had become one of the chief means by which a poet built a reputation and a following, she found the expenditure of nervous energy not worth the product. Furthermore, they caused a disturbance in the normal flow of her life; they took her away from the primary task, which was the making of the poems. If this meant she would publish less and sell fewer copies of those books she published, so be it. This was a decision she made before she was thirty, and she never looked back.

She also made her peace with the Valley. Most of the poets who studied with her at Fresno State—Larry Levis, David St. John, Greg Pape, Gary Soto—got out as soon as they could. Italy may have been where her heart was, but Fresno was where her husband practiced medicine, her children went to school, and she wrote her best poems. For the anthology *The Geography of Home* she wrote a prose introduction to her poems that addressed exactly that.

Over the last thirty years, I have come to learn that two essential components of the celebratory tradition in poetry are passion and careful observation. While I was never lacking in the first, the second was a task made all the more difficult by living in a place that often seemed desolate and impoverished. Difficult, but not impossible. Even now, if you drive east a few miles into the countryside or the nearby foothills, the fields of yellow grass with their outcroppings of rock and skeletal oaks are still reminiscent in their rugged beauty of parts of southern Europe.

If she couldn't live in the Italy she loved, she was determined to find a way of bringing the country of her devotion to the Valley, and she did exactly that with her poetry.

In a singular poem entitled "Geraniums" from her book *The Pilgrim Among Us* she wrote,

> *In the next world, I will be the one*
> *forever pushing open*
> *the warped, green shutters to let*
> *the sunlight enter the room . . .*

I wouldn't be surprised if that was true, but what I know for certain is that in this world Roberta was constantly pushing aside the shutters to let light in. The young woman I encountered over thirty years ago would never let well-enough pass for wisdom. She wanted to know why: Why this word and not that? Why this poem, or any poem at all? My initial impulse was to urge Valium on her, but as that first semester wore on I realized I had someone rare, a truth seeker who let nothing stop her. Over the years of our friendship, whenever I wanted to revive my belief in the value of writing poetry or living a moral life, I would call on Roberta, either in her poetry or in her person, and she was always there for me, as she was for all her brothers and sisters in the art of poetry or the art of life. She wrote once of another being: "There are some creatures, who take / all of history with them / when they kneel one last time / in the hard, bitten grass, / only to come back later / with their sense of life, / their nerve as crisp / as a new apple." Modest as she always was, I'm sure she had no idea she had forged the perfect emblem of her undying spirit.

Her final year was particularly difficult, what with extended bouts of chemo and a month-long stay for a bone-marrow transplant at the Stanford Medical Center. There had been a brief period of remission—one we measured in weeks, not months—and then the resurgence of the illness. I spoke with her on the phone near the end; I'd given her a batch of what to me had been unfamiliar poems by Pavese, both in the original Italian and in the new translations by Geoffrey Brock, and she called to thank me for this invaluable gift. Poetry never lost its importance for her, even with the specter of the end only days away. A year ago last spring the community of poets and poetry readers here in the Valley lost one of its guiding stars. We knew then we lost more than a poet: we lost a radiant friend for life who had enriched our years, a woman of independence and spirit whose vision will continue to sing, moving and touching readers for as long as people care about American poetry.

Roberta Spear died on April 2, 2003.

GETTING AND SPENDING

This talk or lecture or illustrated reading has an odd genesis. When Eileen Mackevich wrote to ask my take on "Saving and Spending," the theme of the 2003 Chicago Humanities Festival, my head began to buzz with several things, and certainly one was a famous sonnet by William Wordsworth, which begins, "The world is too much with us, late and soon, / Getting and spending, we lay waste our powers—; / Little we see in Nature that is ours; / We have given our hearts away, a sordid boon!" I've always responded to those lines with a little shudder. I haven't given my heart away, and I've not been dedicated to a life of getting and spending in the way Wordsworth meant. So I've said to myself each time I encountered the poem, "Speak for yourself, Willy!"

Let me be clear; I love much of the poetry of Wordsworth. His sonnet "Composed Upon Westminster Bridge" was the first great city poem I encountered, when I was eighteen and looking for such poems for the first time, having tired of the rural rhapsodies we encountered in public school; it is a vision of the city at dawn before the commerce of the day can cheapen or dirty it, a vision of beauty where—as a city boy—I figured I'd have to look for it. It includes the gorgeous line "The river glideth at his own sweet will," which thirty-some years later I would use as an epigraph for a collection of poems entitled *Sweet Will*. His great "Ode on Intimations of Immortality" would serve as a model for one of the best poems I ever wrote, "A Walk with Tom Jefferson." The poet-critic Paul Mariani, in an essay on my work, regards Wordsworth as a major influence on my own writing and thinking, and I would have to agree.

And yet I have never liked William Wordsworth as a man. I found him cold, ungiving, someone frightened of spending himself for others, to employ the vocabulary of these events. What, you might ask, brought me to these conclusions?

My first sense of his self-centeredness came during my study of his great contemporary John Keats. In the initial biography I read of Keats there is a scene that is enormously painful to anyone who has come to love the poetry of Keats and the man as well. The scene: The young Keats attends a dinner party where he will for the first time meet one of his early heroes, a man he knows for certain is a great poet. The evening has been arranged by Keats's friend the painter Benjamin Haydon for exactly this purpose: so that Keats can meet Wordsworth. Others of note are invited— the poet John Reynolds, Charles Lamb, Thomas Monkhouse, and the painter John Landseer—and one of them urges Keats to read a recent poem, not one of his best, the "Hymn to Pan" from *Endymion*. The young poet does so. There is silence, and then the great man puts the event in perspective: "A pretty piece of paganism," he remarks, and the young poet is shattered. I carried that scene in my head for twenty years after reading the Keats biography by Sidney Colvin; but in 1963 two superb new biographies appeared, one by Walter Jackson Bate, the other by Aileen Ward, and both corrected my impression and set the record straight. The initial meeting was arranged by Haydon; it took place at the home of Thomas Monkhouse. On the way there, according to Haydon, Keats expressed "the greatest, purest, the most unalloyed pleasure at the prospect" of meeting the poet. Haydon goes on to describe the scene as follows:

"Wordsworth received him kindly, and after a few minutes, Wordsworth asked him what he had been doing lately. I said he has just finished an exquisite ode to Pan—and as he had not a copy I begged Keats to repeat it," which Keats did from memory while pacing the room, no doubt from nervousness; and when he finished, Haydon wrote, "Wordsworth dryly said, 'a very pretty piece of Paganism'—This was unfeeling, and unworthy of his high Genius to a young Worshipper like Keats—and Keats felt it deeply." I should add that Haydon wrote this account precisely because Leigh Hunt had in print placed the introduction and recitation at the famous dinner party. Hunt, not having been invited so as not to distress Wordsworth, might have held a grudge. In any event, the harm was done to my estimation of a great poet, which is to say I have for fifty years believed the scene which most discredits the older poet. Not very giving or generous of me.

Keats seems to have been far more generous; perhaps his confidence was so high in regard to the poem that he wasn't bothered by the remark. After all, shouldn't a hymn to Pan be just that, "a pretty piece of Paganism," Pan being part of a mythological pagan world and not Wordsworth's cosmos, for by this time he was a devout Christian? Keats understood the distance between himself and Wordsworth in regard to their distinct visions of what a poet is. In a letter to his friend Richard Woodhouse, Keats wrote, "As to the poetical Character itself (I mean that sort of which, if I am anything, I am a Member; that sort distinguished from the Wordsworthian or egotistical sublime; which is a thing per se and stands alone) it is not itself—it has no self . . ." He goes on to explain that "a poet is the most unpoetical of any thing in existence; because he has no Identity—he is continually in for—and filling some other Body . . ." Wordsworth had no such identity problem. I say that seriously and in jest, for in truth those of us who regard the writing of Keats as astonishing have come to see this lack of identity as one of his great strengths, without which he would never have been the man or poet he became.

By the way, none of the biographers attempts to explain this mean-spiritedness on the part of Wordsworth, and none of them is surprised by it, for he was at that moment regarded by the literate public and by himself as the greatest living poet. Bate tells us "his scorn of disguising anything and his obstinacy in stating exactly what he thought, even if it showed his own egocentricity," were well known to his friends. Unbending, unyielding, he was a man closing himself off from the world and even from his own early nature. The young Wordsworth was a believer in the almost unlimited potential of the human. He hailed the French Revolution and the throwing-off of the old chains of the monarchy and the people's enslavement to the titled landowners and the church, but that was not the Wordsworth Keats met. That Wordsworth had become what in modern America we call a Republican.

The Keats that Wordsworth met, however, as we see from what I quoted above, was a man who failed to find a distinction between himself and the creatures and beings of the world he inhabited; "if a sparrow come before my window, I take part in its existence and pick about the gravel," he wrote, and in another letter we learn of his joy, his boundless pleasure, in the richness of human diversity. He imagines a world in which we share the great contraries of our mental lives. "An old Man and a child would talk together and the old Man be led on his path, and the child left thinking Man should not dispute or assert but whisper results to his neighbor," and in this way "every human might become great, and Humanity instead of being a wide heath of Furze and Briars with here and there a remote Oak or Pine, would become a grand democracy of Forest Trees!" This vision of the human and the poet's role in the scheme of human development, the poet as spender of the self for the celebration of the world that gives him being, was not something determined by his DNA. The world insofar as he knew it taught him to become John Keats, though granted there was something in his character that made him even in childhood an avid learner, a creature of enormous curiosity and good fellowship as well. To borrow his own terminology, it was the world—his experience of it—that allowed him to transform that world from what others called a "Vale of Tears" into what he called a "Vale of Soul-Making." In his great journal letter of 1819 to his brother George and his sister-in-law in America, he attempts to parse the role of suffering in a scheme of human development. As an apprentice surgeon in a London hospital, he knew the extremes of suffering and pain firsthand. "Call the world if you Please 'The Vale of Soul-making.' Then you will find out the use of the world." He goes on to further define, or perhaps discover, his meaning. "I say 'Soul-making' Soul as distinguished from an Intelligence—There may be Intelligences or sparks of the divinity in millions—but they are not Souls until they acquire identities, till each one is personally itself." And how does this happen? he asks himself. "How, but by the medium of a world like this?" Reading his letters, which are the finest we have by any poet, you come to see that like the best writing in any genre they are acts of discovery. We are witnesses, through the agency of this particular letter, to the very act of the twenty-three-year-old poet formulating one of his most astonishing visions. For example, he remarks that he's not expressing very well what he "but dimly" perceives. He begins again, this time employing the imagery of the classroom: "I will call the *world* a School instituted for the purpose of teaching little children to read—I will call the *human heart* the *horn Book used in that school*—and I will call the *Child* able to read, the Soul." He feels this is a grander system of salvation than that offered by the church, for it makes the world necessary in a "system of Spirit-creation." That essential kernel of the self, the soul, the name we give for our most basic identity, is something we create by means of our experience of the world, and the world is not "the other" but an essential element in the creation of the self. Thus by one's very nature one is "free to pick about the gravel with the sparrow," that always questing creature so much like the poet himself.

Eileen Mackevich's query also brought to mind a brilliant essay by one of the finest American poets of the last several decades, Larry Levis, who died in 1996 at the age of forty-nine and long before he could give us the riches of his mind and imagination. In a portion of an essay he tries to define the essential qualities of his most influential teacher, and in so doing he gives us a road map to his own notion of a person's spiritual and social uses. "What still strikes me as amazing, and right, and sane, was his capacity to share all that energy, that fire, with those around him: students and poets and friends. The only discernible principle I gathered from this kind of generosity seems to be this: to try to conserve one's energy for some later use, to try to teach as if one is not quite there and has more important things to do, is a way to lose that energy completely, a way quite simply of betraying oneself." What Levis seems too kind to say is that it's also a way of betraying one's friends, one's fellow poets, and one's students. Those of us who have been students, teachers, friends officially or simply in the course of living, have observed this conservation of energy far more often than the spending that animated both Levis's teacher and Levis's own writing.

The spending of self which is at the core of both Levis's poetry and his conception of teaching, like Keats's view of the relationship between the poet and what he called the world, takes us into the realm of what today we call "character." It may strike you that I am talking about an area of human nature that in today's corrupted world is reserved for Republicans. Do I suddenly sound like a Republican? Let me sound like a Republican. I should add that neither Keats nor Levis was addicted to gambling or windbaggery. It's only fair to note that selfishness has not stopped people from writing first-rate poetry. You conservative poets out there, don't give up hope. Some true poets have been absolutely genial at exploiting their failures as human beings.

We have some idea of how Keats arrived at the astonishing vision and consummate artistry that gave us in the spring and summer of 1819 the greatest outpouring of lyrical poetry in our language—the great odes. That year saw as well the creation of two of his strongest narrative poems, "Lamia" and "The Eve of St. Agnes," and all we have of his final version of his projected epic, *Hyperion,* this before the poet was twenty-four. One fact we have with surety: young John Keats loved to write; he lived for those times he could sit down at his desk and work at poetry. Near the end of that remarkably creative period, in a letter to his brother George, he wrote: "Whenever I find myself growing vaporish, I rouse myself, wash and put on a clean shirt, brush my hair and clothes, tie my shoestrings neatly, and, in fact, adonize as if I were going out—then, all clean and comfortable, I sit down to write. This I find the greatest relief."

What a refreshing vision of the artist at work, and one

that seems perfectly appropriate to a genius of Keats's moral vision. He knew as surely as he knew anything that his "gift," his genius for poetry, was exactly that, a gift, and nothing he had earned through some inherent merit or collection of deeds; and as it was in its nature a gift, it demanded a repayment to the world, and he put his life in order so that the giver—hap, fortune, the world—might be repaid in full; and given so few years, twenty-five in all, he did better than anyone could ask. Near the end he is reported to have said, "I think I shall be among the immortals," and in truth he already was.

Dead only a brief period in the span of things, Larry Levis has no biography, authorized or otherwise, to help us know how he became himself, but in an autobiographical essay published in 1996, less than a year before he died, he presents us with a fable that in many ways accounts for why he turned to poetry and why he became the particular poet and man he became: in other words, in Keatsian terms, he accounts for the first and most essential step in the construction of his soul. The materials of the fable are drawn expertly from his own experience as a farm worker on his father's ranch near Selma, California, a town known—if it is known at all—as "the Raisin Capital of the World," a place of such overwhelming mediocrity and cultural poverty he knew almost as soon as he took up the pen that he must leave if he was to become a poet. The land, he tells us in his exquisite and hilarious prose, "was a kind of paradise preserved, held intact, by the toxic perfume of malathion and sulfur . . . and by the people who worked on it, who were Mexican if they were older, Chicano if younger, who spoke Spanish mostly, and who were underpaid." He cites an interview with Cesar Chavez late in life when Chavez turned to a journalist and, pointing at a family of farmworkers resting in the shade from their labors, said, "You see? They are so . . . innocent." Levis says he knew what Chavez meant, and yet to Larry they were not a "they," but men he worked with in the orchards, Ignacio Calderon, Johnny Dominguez, Jaime Huerta, Tea, among others, and an older man who ate his lunch alone, rarely spoke, and whom the others called Señor Solo.

The young Levis worked with them summer after summer, and he tells us they teased him with great affection. The nickname they chose for him was Cowboy. "I felt honored to work beside them," he writes, "because I *was* only a boy, and an Anglo boy at that, and the son of the *patrón*." He grew to love their putdowns, delivered usually in Spanish and with a studied formality Levis regarded as "courtliness." He quotes one from memory: "Con su permiso, Jaime, su café no vale tres chingaderas. Pero muchas gracias, sin embargo." ("With your permission, Jimmy, your coffee is not worth three motherfuckers, but I thank you for it with an infinite gratitude nonetheless.") And this, of course, is answered with an even more obscene and riotous response. It is young Levis's first exposure to what urban Americans call the dozens, but delivered with an unusual degree of formality and fluency, something approaching an oral poetry which is easily the equal of what we now witness or ignore at so-called poetry slams.

One young man, Fermin, practiced it with an eloquence and imagination that for the young Levis transformed it into an art. One day Fermin turned his attention to an elderly immigrant from Okinawa, Kijima, who spoke only Japanese. The myth that Fermin invents—in English, for he is equally adept in both Spanish and English—involves the *novia* (bride-to-be) of the elderly Kijima and the sexual circus she took part in with Fermin and the other laborers the night before as they attempted to instruct her in the art of love. This in spite of the fact that Kijima never had a friend of either sex except for a half-blind dog. Everyone laughed outrageously at the wildness and beauty of the extended tale—that is, until the older worker Señor Solo spoke of the unkindness of laughing at the man, humiliating him, even if he didn't understand a word. "Slowly," Levis tells us, "one by one, everyone working in the trees would come down from his ladder and go up to Kijima where he was working and apologize, in Spanish mostly. In my case in English. Kijima had no idea what we were saying to him, but he bowed to each of us and smiled anyway."

For Levis this final ritual was a way of giving back to Kijima the dignity they had stolen from him, a dignity that still exists, Levis writes, on the "outskirts of small towns . . . places where 'executives would never want to tamper,'" as Levis quotes that marvelous phrase from W. H. Auden, a dignity he calls "completely unmarketable in the world." It is of course the dignity that he later finds poetry able to confer when it is used for its highest purposes, to honor all that which is truly alive and ignored in a world like ours. Levis was only twelve or thirteen when he succumbed to this rite of passage into the world of dedication to something indefinable and beautiful, something involving the power and joy in the play of language as an end in itself as well as a means for the construction of a true community among men and women.

Four years later, the only kid in Selma high school who'd heard of T. S. Eliot and read Frost and Stevens, he tried one night to write a poem and promised himself that if it contained one good line he would become a poet. Not "try" to become a poet, he wrote. "You will either be a poet," he told himself, "and become a better and better one, or you will not be a poet." The following morning he looked at the thing he'd written, which in spite of its wretchedness, contained the one good line. "One," he tells us. "All the important decisions in my life were made in that moment."

Two years later he had the good fortune to stumble into the classroom of the teacher who taught him the virtue of spending and the pettiness of saving oneself. He describes his mentor as having "a talent for making the most self-conscious young students laugh at themselves and at their mistakes; by doing so they could suddenly go beyond their useless, narrow, brittle egos they had carried with them since junior high like a life savings in the wrong currency; that laughter woke them from the sleep of adolescence into something far larger. What was larger was the world of poetry, not only the study of it . . . but the possibility of writing it." You could enter into this larger world where "the only president was Imagination."

Notice how with such grace Levis slips into the language of commerce, "a life savings in the wrong currency," as he discovers the limitation of not spending the self and defines the wealth that awaits those who give freely of the self. Describing his mentor, he tells us far more about his own take on the notion of saving and spending than that of his teacher. I sense that any older writer who'd taken Levis seriously would have had the same effect, for in truth this is a narrative of self-discovery more than anything else. "Because we mattered so much to him, we began to matter to ourselves. And to matter in this way, to feel that what one did and how one wrote actually might make a difference, was a crucial gift . . . given to each of us. All you had to do was open it," Levis writes, and "it became quite clear . . . that only cowardice or self-deceit could keep us from doing that"—that is, accepting the gift.

Reading the story of Levis's discovery of the poet within himself, the poet and the profound adventurer in the land of the imagination, it is impossible not to reflect back upon the opportunity that Wordsworth, secure in his reputation and inflated ego, threw away on that first meeting with the young Keats. An opportunity like that comes to very few older writers, and he threw it away in order to make a wisecrack. Fortunately, that young Keats had already discovered who he was and had begun to create his poetic vision. And the great work was soon to follow. So a rare opportunity was lost, not by Keats but by Wordsworth, whose own poetry at that time was becoming more and more of an effort to revise the greatest work of his past, "The Prelude," which he continued to tinker with and emasculate for the rest of his creative life. This failure on Wordsworth's part has become for me an emblem of how we lose what is most precious in the act of saving oneself from the expenditure of feeling and the uncertainty involved in risking the self.

Later in my reading I would encounter a similar warning in the poetry of D. H. Lawrence. In his great poem "Snake," Lawrence depicts himself coming upon a snake in rural Sicily, a creature he's heard is poisonous. He listens to the voices of his "accursed human education," hurls a stick at the creature, which disappears down a hole. Immediately Lawrence regrets the act and wishes the snake would return, for it seems now to him an uncrowned king of the underworld. The poem ends:

> And so, I missed my chance with one of the lords
> Of life.
> And I have something to expiate:
> A pettiness.

I repeat to myself often: You only get so many chances with the lords of life; don't lose them by saving yourself.

•

I've gone on at some length regarding the phrase "getting and spending" from the great Wordsworth sonnet, and spoken mostly about the half devoted to spending and how the two poets Levis and Keats valued the spending of the self in the effort to create themselves and their art. Never for a moment think they were merely innocent children living in a world that would soon kill them. Keats was a man of great pluck and a terrific battler for the well-being of the underdog, and in one famous case the underdog was just that, a small dog being whipped by a butcher outraged by some doggy infraction. Though barely over five feet in height, and slender, Keats took the man on in a battle of fisticuffs that ended only with the release of the dog from his torturer. He was an immensely attractive human being; even as a boy he found people drawn to him. Like Levis, he had the good fortune to encounter a sympathetic teacher, John Clarke, who had given up the profession of law in order to do something more congenial to his personality. Here is how Clarke describes the young Keats: "He was not merely the favorite of all, like a pet prize-fighter, for his terrier courage; but his high-mindedness, his utter unconsciousness of a mean motive, his placability, his generosity, wrought so general a feeling in his behalf that I never heard a word of disapproval from any one, superior or equal, who had known him."

Getting was a preoccupation of his short life, for he was the oldest of the four children of Thomas Keats, a "livery-stable keeper" who died in a fall from a horse when John was only eight. Within six years his mother died, probably from tuberculosis, the disease that would wipe out John and his two brothers; from the age of sixteen he was constantly concerned with the welfare of the four, and hence he trained to become a surgeon. Reading his life one is struck by the fact he had no adolescence; he could afford none.

Levis, the youngest of four children, grew up in a large and stable family, and though in a backwater town, he knew the attractions of wealth and power; but what he went about "getting" (to use Wordsworth's term) was a poetic voice powerful enough to carry his vision of the world. Nothing America offered in its immense array of baubles could tempt him away from that striving for inner wealth. Like Keats, he was surrounded by a circle of friends who attested to his genius, his outrageous sense of humor (the poet David St. John called him the funniest person he'd ever met)—his utter lack of that competitive smallness that haunts the narrow halls of the house of poetry, his candor, and especially his electric presence. He loved motorcycles, and I'm glad to say that before he was forty he was able to afford a Harley Sportster, which played no part in his early death and was his only expensive indulgence. He spoke often of having to live on the edge in order to keep his senses alive, and he believed he required that alertness to entertain the poetry he meant to create. The degree to which he committed himself to his poetry is almost frightening. He believed that is what poetry demanded, a total commitment, a relentless gathering of whatever can be transformed by the alchemy of the imagination into the metal of poetry.

Near the end of that remarkable season of Keats's life that his biographer Robert Gittings called "the Living Year" and Walter Jackson Bate "the Fertile Year," Keats wrote what many believe is the most beautiful poem in the language, "To Autumn." For the present purposes, it is fascinating to compare it to another utterly remarkable poem dealing with the same season, this one by a little-known sixteenth-century English poet, Thomas Nashe, a contemporary of Shakespeare.

> *AUTUMN hath all the summer's fruitful treasure ;*
> *Gone is our sport, fled is poor Croydon's pleasure.*
> *Short days, sharp days, long nights come on apace,—*
> *Ah, who shall hide us from the winter's face?*
> *Cold doth increase, the sickness will not cease,*
> *And here we lie, God knows, with little ease.*
> > *From winter, plague, and pestilence, good Lord*
> > *deliver us!*
>
> *London doth mourn, Lambeth is quite forlorn ;*
> *Trades cry, Woe worth that ever they were born.*
> *The want of term is town and city's harm ;*
> *Close chambers we do want to keep us warm.*
> *Long banished must we live from our friends ;*
> *This low-built house will bring us to our ends.*
> > *From winter, plague, and pestilence, good Lord*
> > *deliver us!*

The expression "the want of term" refers to the absence of any sure or fixed income; both Lambeth and Croydon were at that time neighborhoods of the poor. The poem is a striking elegy for the end of a season of joy and plenty, the summer, which in England—dreary as we may conceive it—is the richest time of the year, a time when nature allows even the destitute a relief from the actual: the constant press of cold, sickness, and of course death. The summer voices of traveling tradesmen Nashe transforms into cries of anguish to the unlistening sky, and the very home that gives shelter, "this low-built house"—low-built to conserve what little heat there is—is likened to that final low-built house, the grave. Nashe, a controversial figure of his age, a pamphleteer, playwright, novelist, and political radical, knew poverty firsthand, and his poem, instead of glorifying the season, regards it as the omen of what is to follow: the coming of winter, the year's culmination in disease and worse. He lived to be only thirty-one and sadly left us only a handful of poems, all of which are masterful. In my reading I've only encountered one autumn poem comparable to Nashe's, and that is Keats's.

TO AUTUMN

Season of mists and mellow fruitfulness,
    Close bosom-friend of the maturing sun;
Conspiring with him how to load and bless
    With fruit the vines that round the thatch-eaves run;
To bend with apples the moss'd cottage-trees,
    And fill all fruit with ripeness to the core;
        To swell the gourd, and plump the hazel shells
    With a sweet kernel; to set budding more,
And still more, later flowers for the bees,
Until they think warm days will never cease,
        For summer has o'er-brimm'd their clammy cells.

Who hath not seen thee oft amid thy store?
    Sometimes whoever seeks abroad may find
Thee sitting careless on a granary floor,
    Thy hair soft-lifted by the winnowing wind;

Or on a half-reap'd furrow sound asleep,
  Drowsed with the fume of poppies, while thy hook
    Spares the next swath and all its twined flowers:
And sometimes like a gleaner thou dost keep
  Steady thy laden head across a brook;
  Or by a cider-press, with patient look,
    Thou watchest the last oozings, hours by hours.

Where are the songs of Spring? Ay, where are they?
  Think not of them, thou hast thy music too,—
While barred clouds bloom the soft-dying day,
  And touch the stubble-plains with rosy hue;
Then in a wailful choir the small gnats mourn
  Among the river sallows, borne aloft
    Or sinking as the light wind lives or dies;
And full grown lambs loud bleat from hilly bourn;
  Hedge-crickets sing; and now with treble soft
  The redbreast whistles from a garden-croft,
    And gathering swallows twitter in the skies.

Unlike the first stanza of the Nashe poem, the opening movement of "To Autumn" does not look ahead. It looks into the present itself and as deeply as possible, and what it finds is not stasis, for the natural processes go on even as they overflow—Keats himself used the term "stationing" to describe this conflation of fullness and growth. In the second stanza the harvester appears, an embodiment of the season, who curiously enough is not harvesting but simply sitting careless or drowsing in a drugged state of fulfillment, patiently watching the last oozings of the cider press. How quietly the suggestion of what must lie ahead enters the poem, and how modest the personification of autumn! In truth the stanza seems to exist in a dream state in which the season as goddess floats in a condition of timeless sensual fulfillment. In the poem's final movement the passage of time enters, as it always does in Keats's poems, as the stanza first looks back to spring and then to what will be: the soft-dying day, the mourning of the gnats, and as the lambs—full-grown now—"bleat from hilly bourn," what is seen fades in the failing light to be replaced in the poem by what is heard in the spreading darkness.

Keats's senses, always keen, seem here even beyond his usual powers as they catch the music borne on the winds, then the songs of the hedge crickets, until the birds gather at last for their necessary voyage toward survival. The fullness of the writing feels extraordinarily appropriate to the moment, for the language and the music of the language, the form itself *is* the poem. Unlike the other odes, there is no poet antagonist present. The first-person pronouns are absent. Each of the other odes presents the poet in a sustained adversarial role, searching for some dramatic resolution to a human problem, such as that posed by the urn with its false sense of a permanence in human affairs, or the song of the nightingale with its suggestion of a flight from the ravages of time. It is almost as though at the moment of Keats's supreme artistry the individual ego merged with the objects that it beheld, and the beholding itself became the poetry. The gifts given by all that lives and dies in time gave birth to the gift that is this supreme poem.

As contemporary readers and writers we ask ourselves: What if there is no one there to receive the gift of the poet's dedication and labors? What if the gift is enormous, a vision by which a people might live, and almost no one chooses to regard it? The nation, the people—who after all are the nation—go about in a frenzy of getting and spending in the crassest and most mindless manner possible, and the great books sit on the shelf or at best are dissected in graduate seminars at Yale and Duke alongside their equivalent texts from Marvel Comics, only deprived of blaring illustrations? In other words, What if the poet is living in today's America? Does the grass stop growing merely because it's part of the White House lawn? Do lovers stop loving because Time Warner sees them only as consumers, or the Department of Defense—once properly called the War Department—regards them as expendable, trash to be, like last year's obsolete weaponry? No, the grass grows and dies and comes back again—unless it's in Selma, California, and an extra ton of malathion kills it forever; the lovers go on with their sacred work—as the poet Rilke regarded their nightly efforts—and the poets write, but of course the nature of what they write changes remarkably, for the true poets among us are not mindless parsnips "frozen in the weather." Even Wordsworth, my bête noir for the duration of this talk, can be described as merely human and different only in our articulation. To say "merely human" is of course to say a great deal; it is to say worthy of standing among all that lives and dies, and of those there is no higher. Poets are men and women with exactly the emotions you have, only they're gifted with more resourcefulness in expressing those feelings in language. So if you're feeling outraged at your career or your country, don't expect them to feel otherwise.

In his marvelous poem "Whitman," Levis speaks in the persona of the father of American poetry but in the vocabulary of the present, a Whitman come back to see what we have done with his country, the one that he and William Blake and Emily Dickinson bequeathed a soul to. Almost as a warning as to the direction the poem will take,

Levis supplies us with two epigraphs from Whitman: the first from *Democratic Vistas*—"I say we had better look our nation searchingly in the face, like a physician diagnosing some deep disease"—the second from the end of his greatest poem, *Song of Myself*—"Look for me under your boot-soles." The key word here is "look," for if we fail to look we will fail to find, and failing to find we will fail to complete ourselves. Let me remind you exactly how *Song of Myself* ends.

> *I bequeath myself to the dirt to grow from the grass I*
> *   love,*
> *If you want me again look for me under your*
> *   boot-soles.*

> *You will hardly know who I am or what I mean,*
> *But I shall be good health to you nevertheless,*
> *And filter and fibre your blood.*
> *Failing to fetch me at first keep encouraged,*
> *Missing me one place search another,*
> *I stop somewhere waiting for you.*

If you live intensely with that great poem, if you reenact it in your imagination, then by the time you intone those lines Walt Whitman is no longer merely Walt, one of the roughs; he has become the spirit of a nation you want to be part of; in searching for the kernel of Whitman you find your deepest self. He spent his life to discover himself in poetry, and he found us.

The Whitman Levis presents us in the poem of that name seems ordinary at first, another American writer consigned to oblivion. I could say that Levis abandons his own voice to enter that of Whitman—for it is Walt who speaks in the poem—but the moment you enter the poem you hear the voice of Levis and not Whitman.

W H I T M A N

I say we had better look our nation searchingly in the face,
like a physician diagnosing some deep disease.

D E M O C R A T I C   V I S T A S

Look for me under your boot-soles.

On Long Island, they moved my clapboard house
Across a turnpike, & then felt so guilty they
Named a shopping center after me!

Now that I'm required reading in your high schools,
Teenagers call me a fool.
Now what I sang stops breathing.

And yet
It was only when everyone stopped believing in me
That I began to live again—
First in the thin whine of Montana fence wire,
Then in the transparent, cast-off garments hung
In the windows of the poorest families,
Then in the glad music of Charlie Parker.
At times now,
I even come back to watch you
From the eyes of a taciturn boy at Malibu.
Across the counter at the beach concession stand,

I sell you hot dogs, Pepsis, cigarettes—
My blond hair long, greasy, & swept back
In a vain old ducktail, deliciously
Out of style.
And no one notices.
Once, I even came back as me,
An aging homosexual who ran the Tilt-a-Whirl
At county fairs, the chilled paint on each gondola
Changing color as it picked up speed,
And a Mardi Gras tattoo on my left shoulder.
A few of you must have seen my photographs,
For when you looked back,
I thought you caught the meaning of my stare:

Still water,
Merciless.

A Kosmos. One of the roughs.

And Charlie Parker's grave outside Kansas City
Covered with weeds.

Leave me alone.
A father who's outlived his only child.

To find me now will cost you everything.

The Walt Whitman shopping center does exist. You enter it from an eight-lane freeway on which no one—hopefully—is reading *Song of Myself.* Once the poet's house was gone, the next thing America set about was the murder of the poet's words, and that was simple: they made him assigned reading. And the song died, but the spirit came back: at first in the music of a fence wire—what stupendous irony, for the fencing-off was a major part of the buying and selling of America—then in the worn clothing of the poor, and before Whitman as himself reenters the nation he sings in the "glad music of Charlie Parker." What an extraordinary adjective to apply to the complex and blues-based inventions of Bird, and how perfectly right! Does it strike you as odd that Levis brings the poet back as a lowly clerk at a concession stand or an aging roustabout working at county fairs? It shouldn't, for the Whitman Levis has given us is a man who has taken his own advice as presented in the introduction to the second edition of *Leaves of Grass*. In this passage he addresses the generations of American poets to come:

> This is what you shall do: Love the earth and sun and
> the animals, despise riches, give alms to every one that
> asks, stand up for the stupid and crazy, devote your
> income and labor to others, hate tyrants . . . take off
> your hat to nothing known or unknown or to any man
> or number of men, go freely with powerful uneducated
> persons and with the young and with the mothers of
> families . . . re-examine all you have been told at school
> or church or in any book, dismiss whatever insults your
> own soul, and your very flesh shall be a great poem . . .

For a moment in history we had his great song with us, and we lost it again in what Delmore Schwartz once called "the scrimmage of appetite." Of course Whitman's vision is still attainable, but as a nation America won't reclaim it with ease or cheaply. And of course we won't buy it back; it's not for sale. That spirit lived in Levis and lives now in the work of our artists, the best of whom have utterly no voice in the career of the nation. To put it in the language of this occasion, the poets spend themselves and America doesn't buy.

Poetry is like truth: on one level it simply is, and as such it is available to anyone. Anyone, that is, who will spend himself or herself to receive it, for no one has an inherent right to truth. One must earn it, and one earns the truth by honoring it, by treasuring it in a thousand daily acts, by shaping one's life to both give it and receive it. The emperors have their treasures, and we have ours. Levis said it perfectly when he spoke in the voice of Whitman, which is the voice of American poetry: "To find me now will cost you everything."

ACKNOWLEDGMENTS

Special thanks to Ann Close, Phil's excellent editor and friend at Knopf. Thanks also to Deborah Landau, the director of the Creative Writing Program at New York University, where Phil completed his long career teaching poetry. I owe a special debt to the gifted young poet Elisa Gonzalez, who unearthed a few of the pieces and worked with me on every aspect of this book. It is more fully realized because of her. My greatest thanks is to Franny Levine, Phil's inspiration and bedrock, who entrusted us with this volume.

Here are the sources for the pieces in this book:

"My Lost Poets" was the 2012 United States Poet Laureate address.

"Nobody's Detroit" appeared in *Detroit Disassembled* (Damiani/Akron Art Museum, 2010) by Andrew Moore.

"On Finding William Carlos Williams and My Poetry" appeared in *Paterson Literary Review*, issue 34 (2005).

"Detroit Jazz in the Late Forties and Early Fifties" appeared in *Ask Me Now: Conversations on Jazz and Literature* (Indiana University Press, 2007) and was originally published in *Brilliant Corners* I, no. 2 (summer 1997).

"A History of My Befuddlement" was the 2009 Judith Lee Stronach Memorial Lecture on the Teaching of Poetry at the Morrison Library at the University of California, Berkeley. The lecture was also published as a booklet in 2010 (Bancroft Library, UC Berkeley).

"A Day in May" appeared in *The Georgia Review* 59, no. 1 (spring 2005).

"A Means of Transport: George Hitchcock and *kayak*" appeared in *Poets & Writers* (May/June 2003).

"The Spanish Civil War in Poetry" was the 1999 ALBA–Bill Sennett Lecture, sponsored by the Bancroft Library, UC Berkeley.

"In the Next World: The Poetry of Roberta Spear" appeared in *Great River Review*, issue 45 (spring/summer 2005), and as the introduction to Roberta Spear's *A Sweetness Rising: New and Selected Poems* (Heyday Books, 2007).

An early version of "Getting and Spending" was delivered as a lecture at the 2003 Chicago Humanities Festival under the title " 'The World is Too Much With Us': Poetry and Spending."

A NOTE ABOUT THE AUTHOR

Philip Levine was born in 1928 in Detroit. He was formally educated in public schools and at Wayne University (now Wayne State University). After a succession of industrial jobs in Detroit, he left the city for good, first attending the writing workshop at the University of Iowa, where he received an MFA in 1957. He then lived in various parts of the country before settling in Fresno, California, where he taught at the state university until his retirement. He also taught in many other places, including Columbia; Princeton; Brown; the University of California, Berkeley; and New York University, where he served as poet in residence for over a decade.

He received many awards for his books of poems, including two National Book Awards—in 1980 for *Ashes: Poems Old and New* and in 1991 for *What Work Is*—and the Pulitzer Prize in 1995 for *The Simple Truth.* He also won the Ruth Lilly Prize in Poetry and the Wallace Stevens Award. In 2006 he was elected a chancellor of the Academy of American Poets, and in 2011 was appointed poet laureate of the United States.

After he retired from teaching at California State University, Fresno, in 1992, he divided his time between Fresno, California, and Brooklyn, New York. He died in 2015.

A NOTE ON THE TYPE

This book was set in Adobe Garamond. Designed for the Adobe Corporation by Robert Slimbach, the fonts are based on types first cut by Claude Garamond (c. 1480–1561). Garamond was a pupil of Geoffroy Tory and is believed to have followed the Venetian models, although he introduced a number of important differences, and it is to him that we owe the letter we now know as "old style." He gave to his letters a certain elegance and feeling of movement that won their creator an immediate reputation and the patronage of Francis I of France.

COMPOSED BY NORTH MARKET STREET GRAPHICS,
LANCASTER, PENNSYLVANIA

PRINTED AND BOUND BY BERRYVILLE GRAPHICS,
BERRYVILLE, VIRGINIA

DESIGNED BY IRIS WEINSTEIN